This Book Belongs to :

_____

_____

_____

Today I am grateful for . . . .

_____
_____
_____
_____
_____
_____
_____
_____
_____
_____
_____
_____
_____
_____
_____
_____

My favorite part of today was . . .

_____
_____
_____
_____
_____
_____
_____
_____
_____
_____
_____

How are you Feeling?

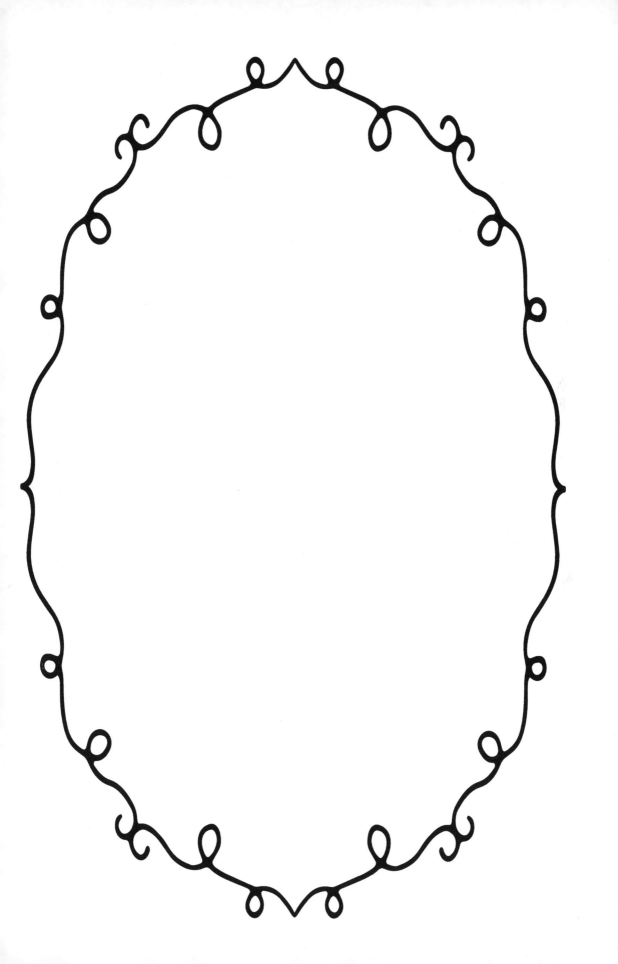

Today I am grateful for . . . .

My favorite part of today was . . .

How are you Feeling?

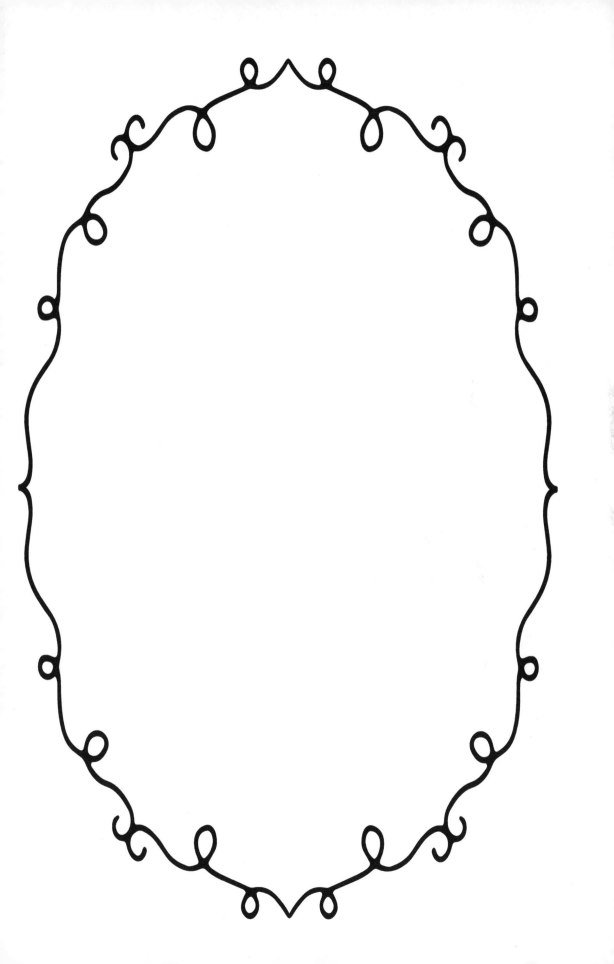

Today I am grateful for . . . .
_____
_____
_____
_____
_____
_____
_____
_____
_____
_____
_____
_____
_____

My favorite part of today was . . .
_____
_____
_____
_____
_____
_____
_____
_____
_____
_____
_____

How are you
Feeling?

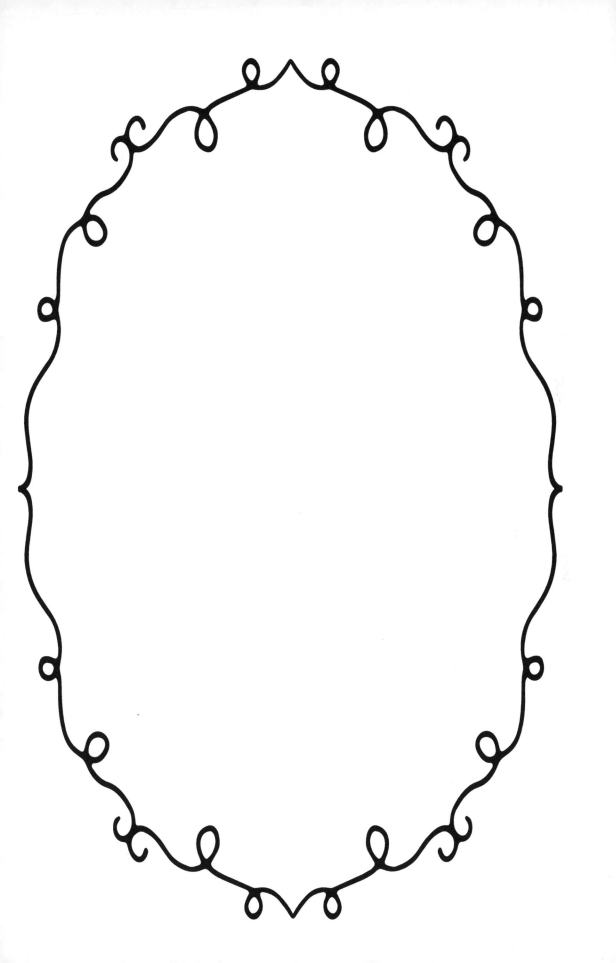

Today I am grateful for . . . .

_____
_____
_____
_____
_____
_____
_____
_____
_____
_____
_____
_____
_____
_____
_____

My favorite part of today was . . .

_____
_____
_____
_____
_____
_____
_____
_____
_____
_____
_____
_____

How are you Feeling?

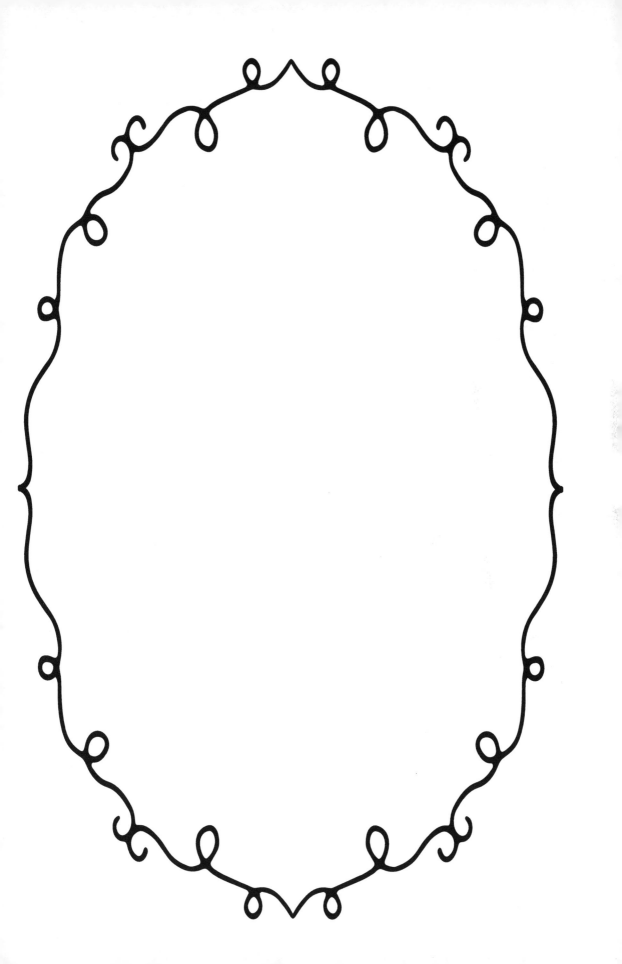

Today I am grateful for . . . .

_____
_____
_____
_____
_____
_____
_____
_____
_____
_____
_____
_____
_____
_____
_____

My favorite part of today was . . .
_____
_____
_____
_____
_____
_____
_____
_____
_____
_____
_____

How are you
Feeling?

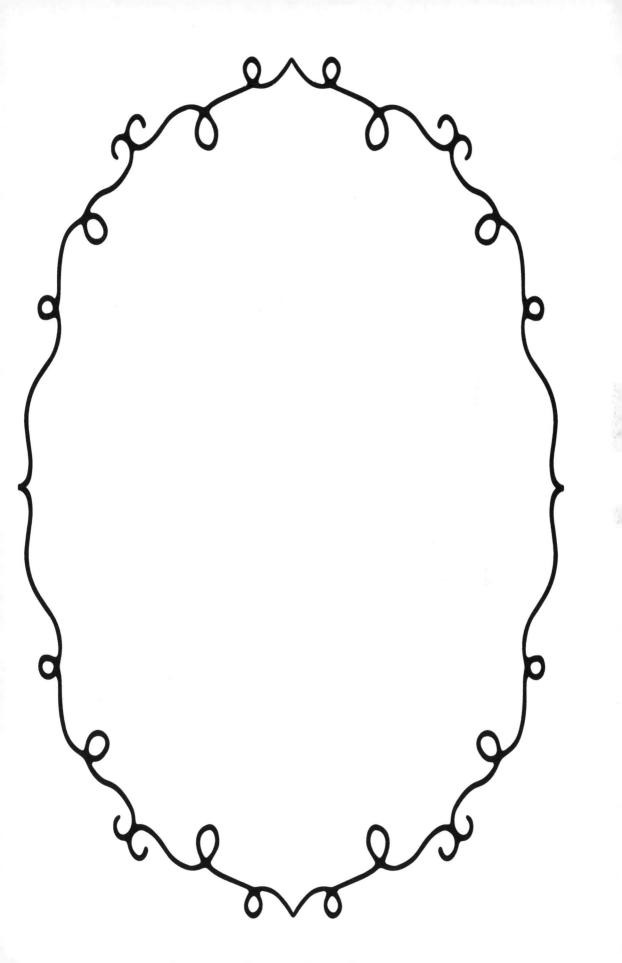

Today I am grateful for . . . .

My favorite part of today was . . .

How are you
Feeling?

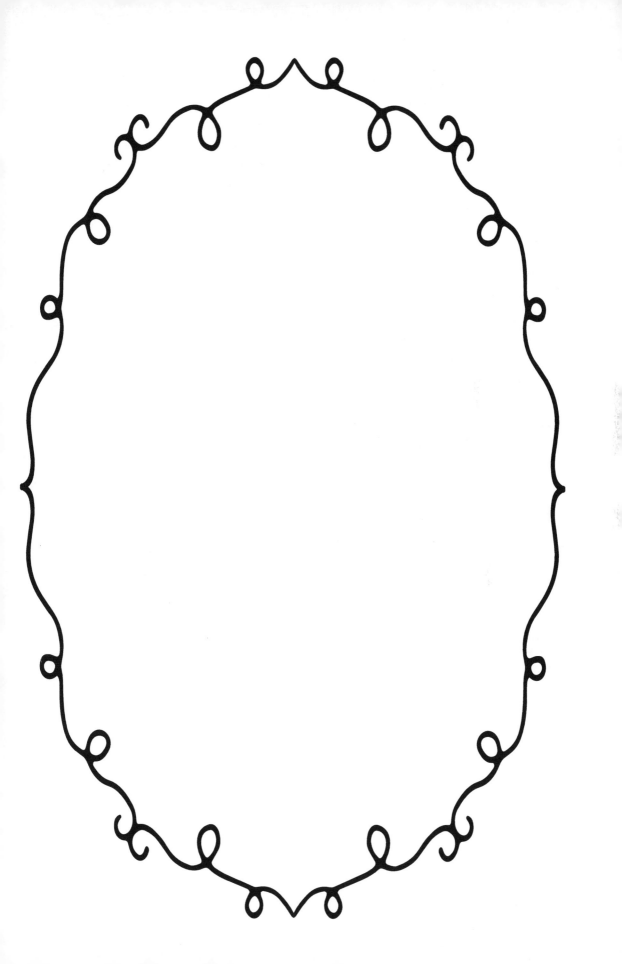

Today I am grateful for . . . .
_____
_____
_____
_____
_____
_____
_____
_____
_____
_____
_____
_____
_____
_____

My favorite part of today was . . .
_____
_____
_____
_____
_____
_____
_____
_____
_____
_____
_____

How are you
Feeling?

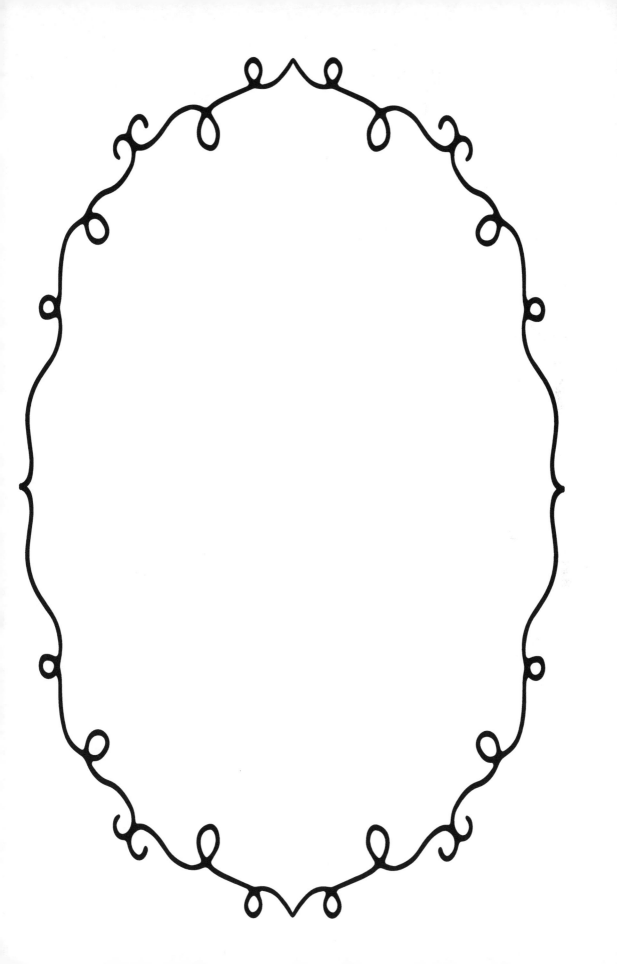

Today I am grateful for . . . .

My favorite part of today was . . .

How are you
Feeling?

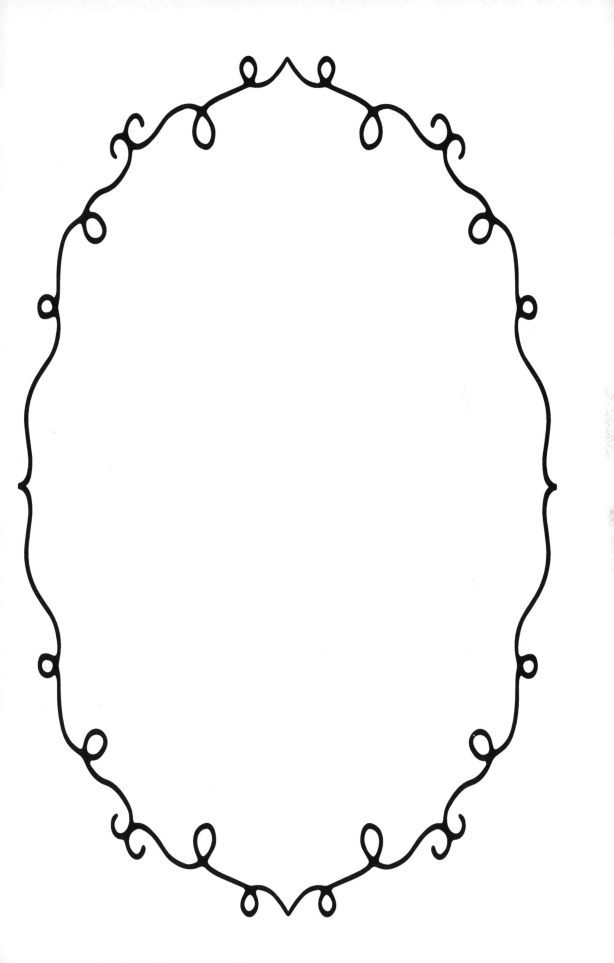

Today I am grateful for . . . .

_____
_____
_____
_____
_____
_____
_____
_____
_____
_____
_____
_____
_____
_____

My favorite part of today was . . .

_____
_____
_____
_____
_____
_____
_____
_____
_____
_____
_____

How are you Feeling?

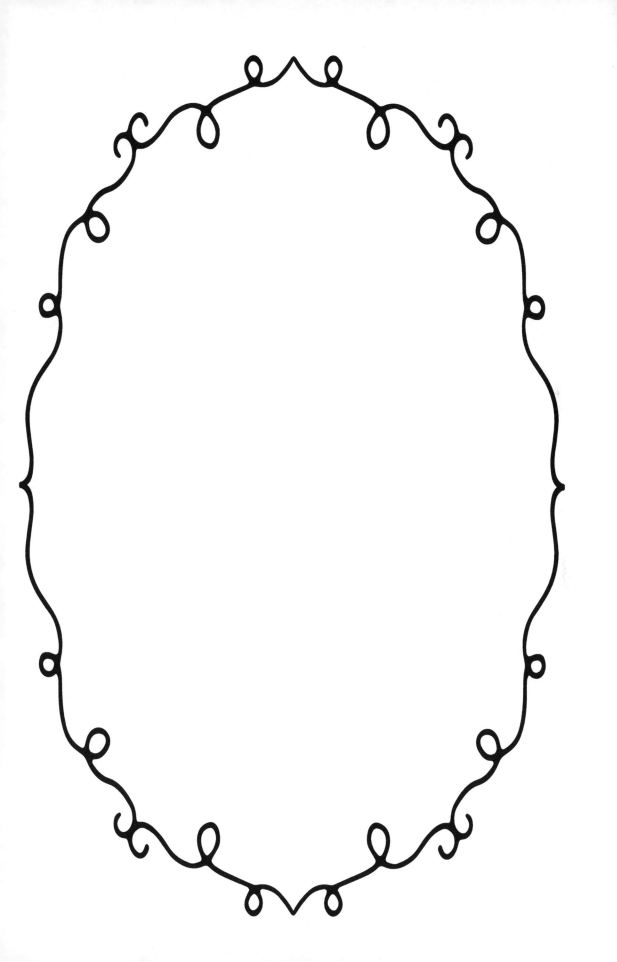

Today I am grateful for . . . .
_____
_____
_____
_____
_____
_____
_____
_____
_____
_____
_____
_____
_____
_____
_____
_____

My favorite part of today was . . .
_____
_____
_____
_____
_____
_____
_____
_____
_____
_____
_____
_____

How are you
Feeling?

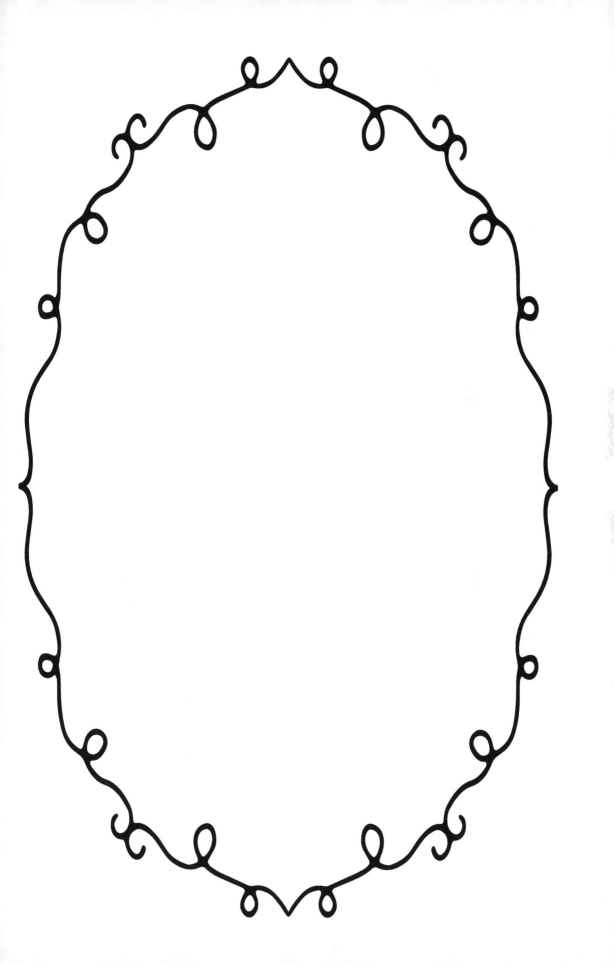

Today I am grateful for . . . .

_____
_____
_____
_____
_____
_____
_____
_____
_____
_____
_____
_____
_____
_____
_____
_____
_____

My favorite part of today was . . .

_____
_____
_____
_____
_____
_____
_____
_____
_____
_____
_____

How are you
Feeling?

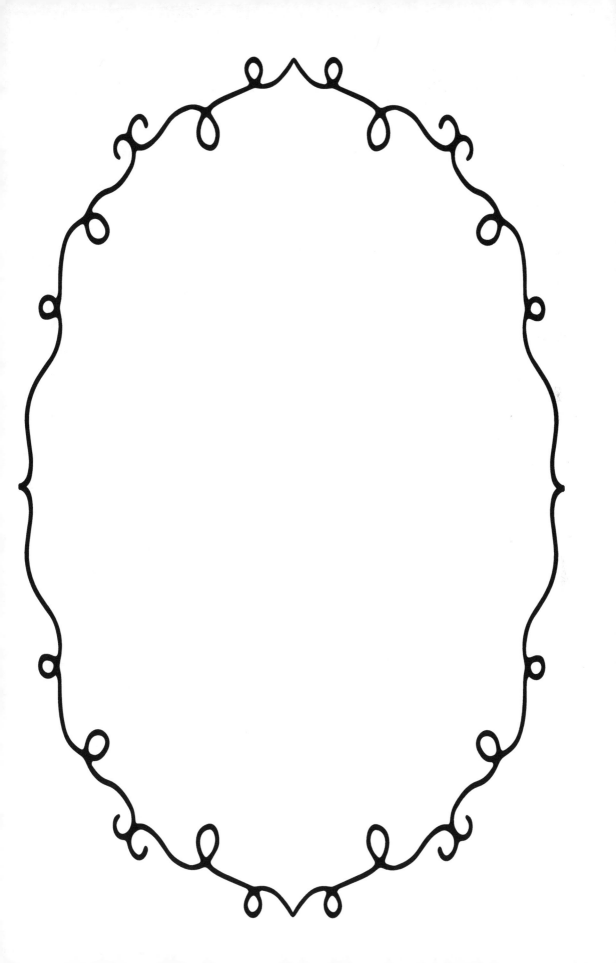

Today I am grateful for . . . .

_____
_____
_____
_____
_____
_____
_____
_____
_____
_____
_____
_____
_____

My favorite part of today was . . .

_____
_____
_____
_____
_____
_____
_____
_____
_____
_____

How are you Feeling?

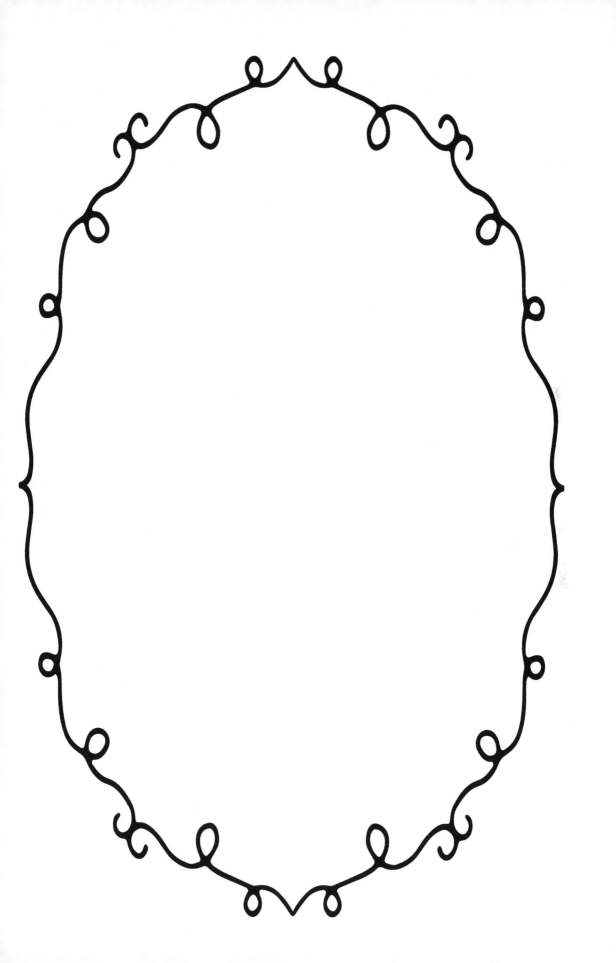

Today I am grateful for . . . .
_____
_____
_____
_____
_____
_____
_____
_____
_____
_____
_____
_____
_____
_____
_____
_____

My favorite part of today was . . .
_____
_____
_____
_____
_____
_____
_____
_____
_____
_____
_____
_____

How are you
Feeling?

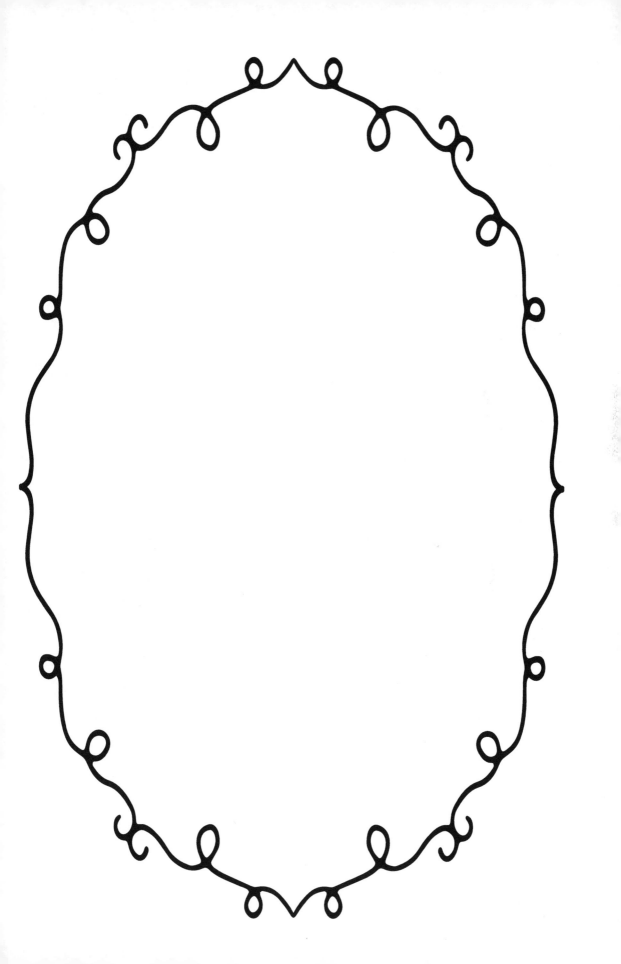

Today I am grateful for . . . .
_____
_____
_____
_____
_____
_____
_____
_____
_____
_____
_____
_____
_____
_____

My favorite part of today was . . .
_____
_____
_____
_____
_____
_____
_____
_____
_____
_____
_____

How are you Feeling?

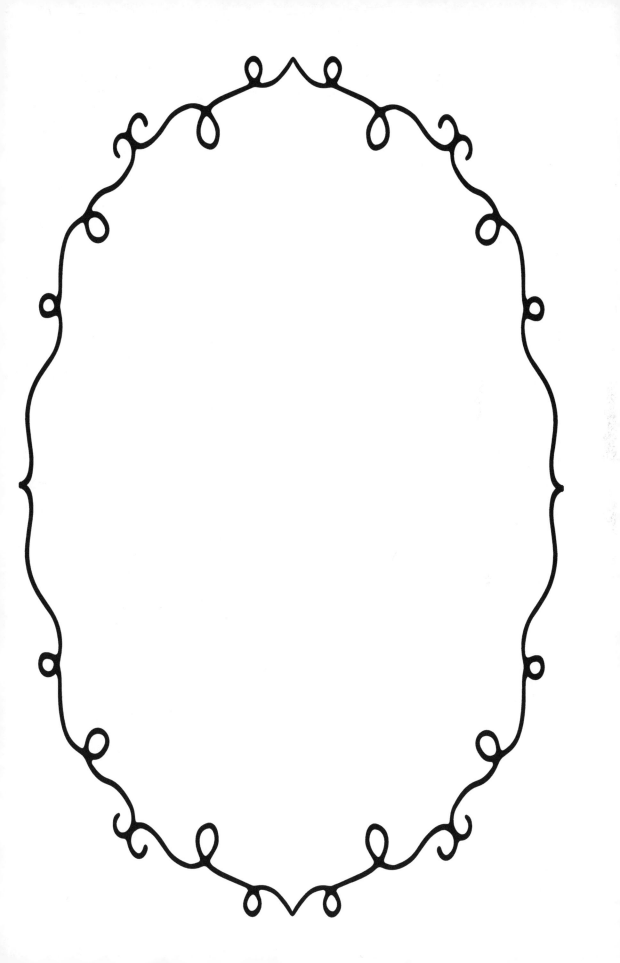

Today I am grateful for . . . .

_____
_____
_____
_____
_____
_____
_____
_____
_____
_____
_____
_____
_____
_____

My favorite part of today was . . .

_____
_____
_____
_____
_____
_____
_____
_____
_____
_____
_____

How are you Feeling?

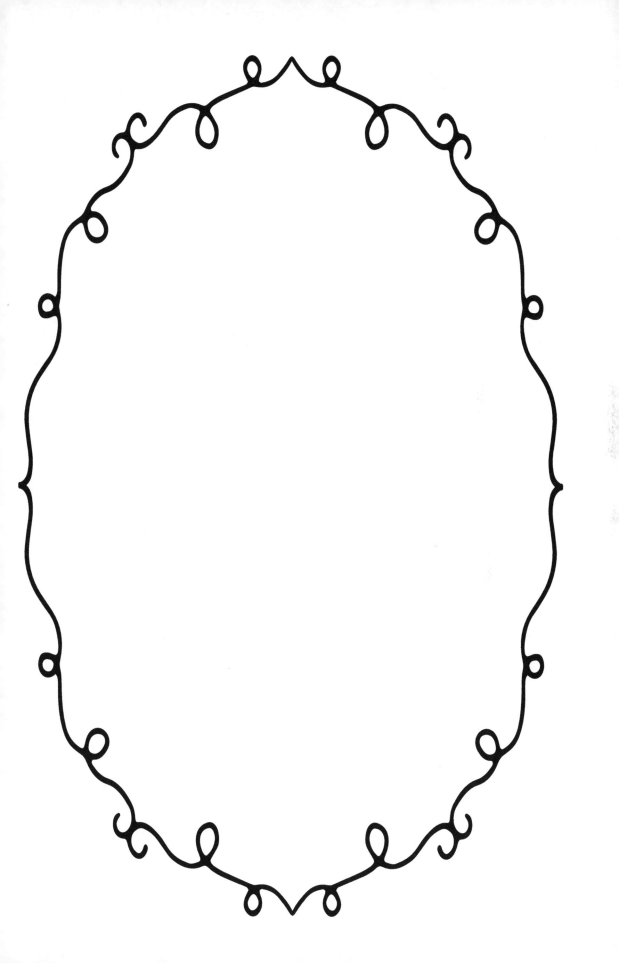

Today I am grateful for . . . .

My favorite part of today was . . .

How are you
Feeling?

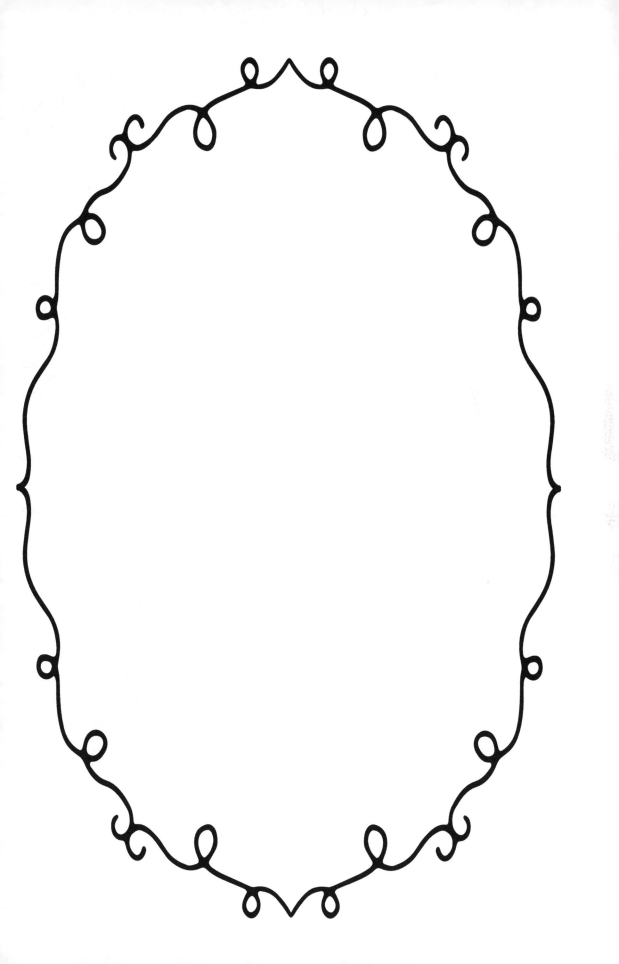

Today I am grateful for . . . .
_____
_____
_____
_____
_____
_____
_____
_____
_____
_____
_____
_____
_____
_____
_____

My favorite part of today was . . .
_____
_____
_____
_____
_____
_____
_____
_____
_____
_____
_____
_____

How are you
Feeling?

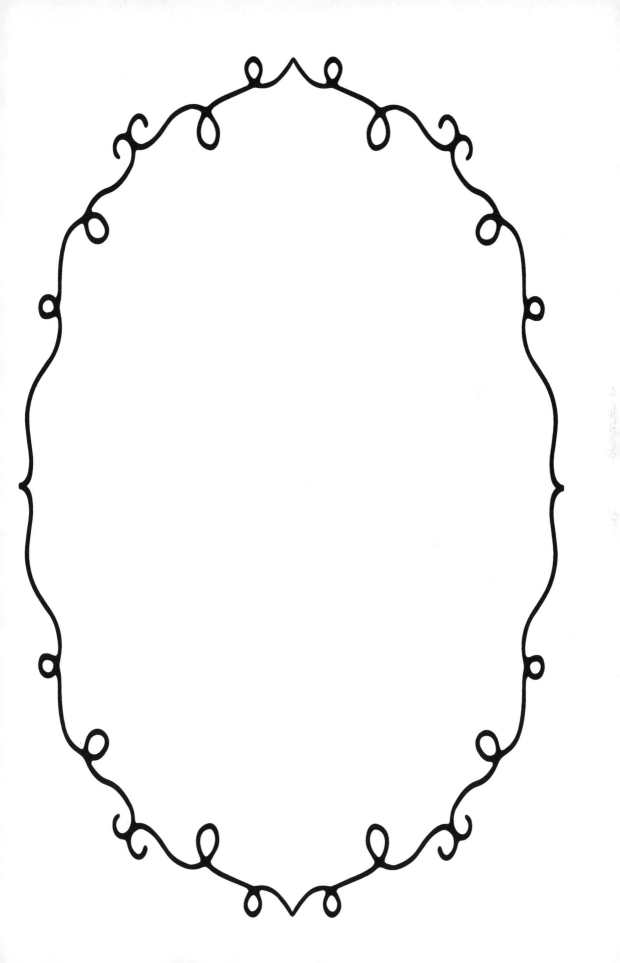

Today I am grateful for . . . .
_____
_____
_____
_____
_____
_____
_____
_____
_____
_____
_____
_____
_____
_____
_____

My favorite part of today was . . .
_____
_____
_____
_____
_____
_____
_____
_____
_____
_____
_____
_____

How are you
Feeling?

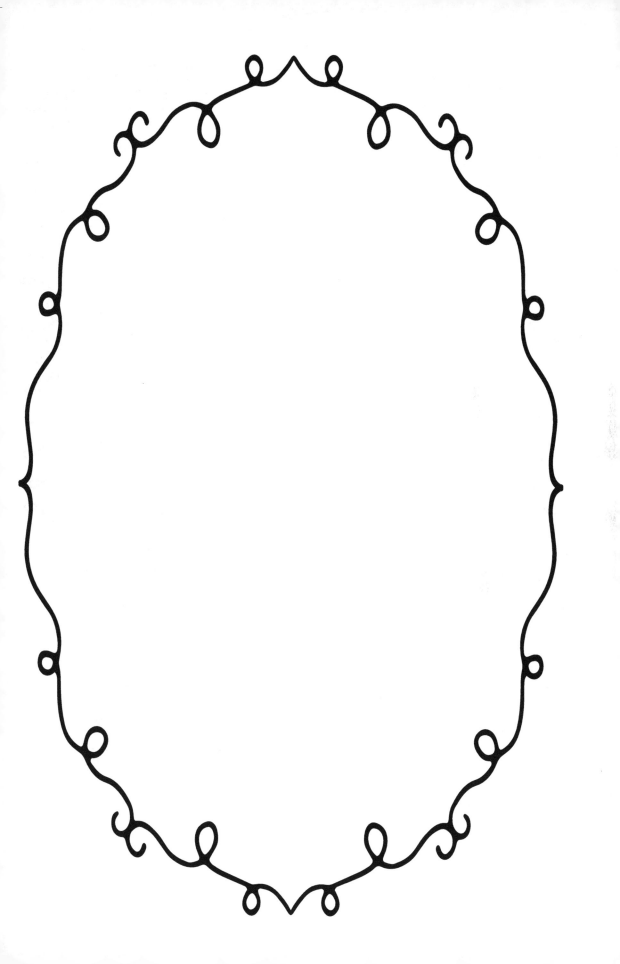

Today I am grateful for . . . .
_____
_____
_____
_____
_____
_____
_____
_____
_____
_____
_____
_____
_____
_____
_____

My favorite part of today was . . .
_____
_____
_____
_____
_____
_____
_____
_____
_____
_____
_____
_____

How are you
Feeling?

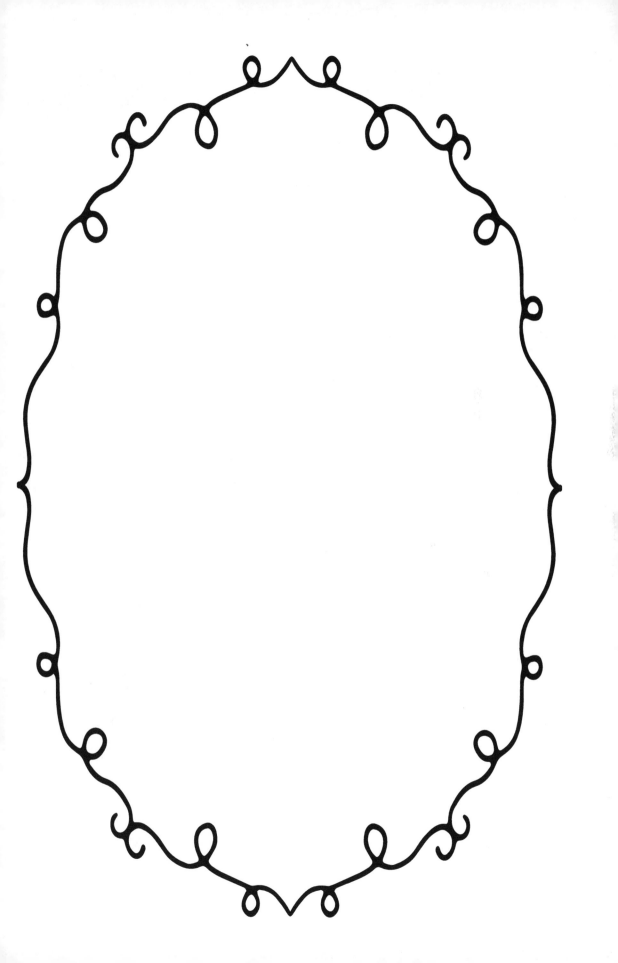

Today I am grateful for . . . .
_____
_____
_____
_____
_____
_____
_____
_____
_____
_____
_____
_____
_____

My favorite part of today was . . .
_____
_____
_____
_____
_____
_____
_____
_____
_____
_____

How are you Feeling?

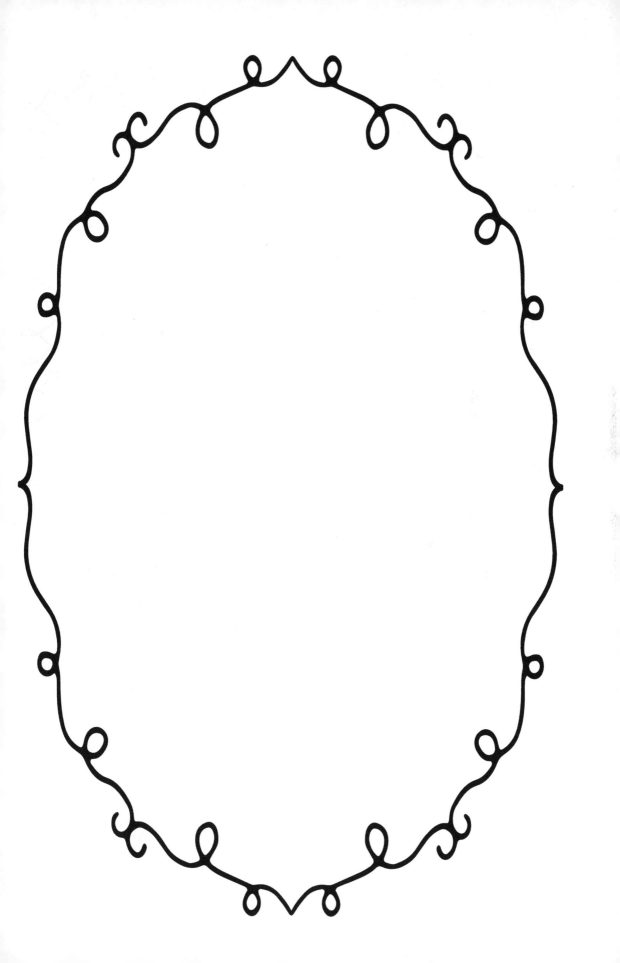

Today I am grateful for . . . .
_____
_____
_____
_____
_____
_____
_____
_____
_____
_____
_____
_____
_____

My favorite part of today was . . .
_____
_____
_____
_____
_____
_____
_____
_____
_____
_____
_____

How are you Feeling?

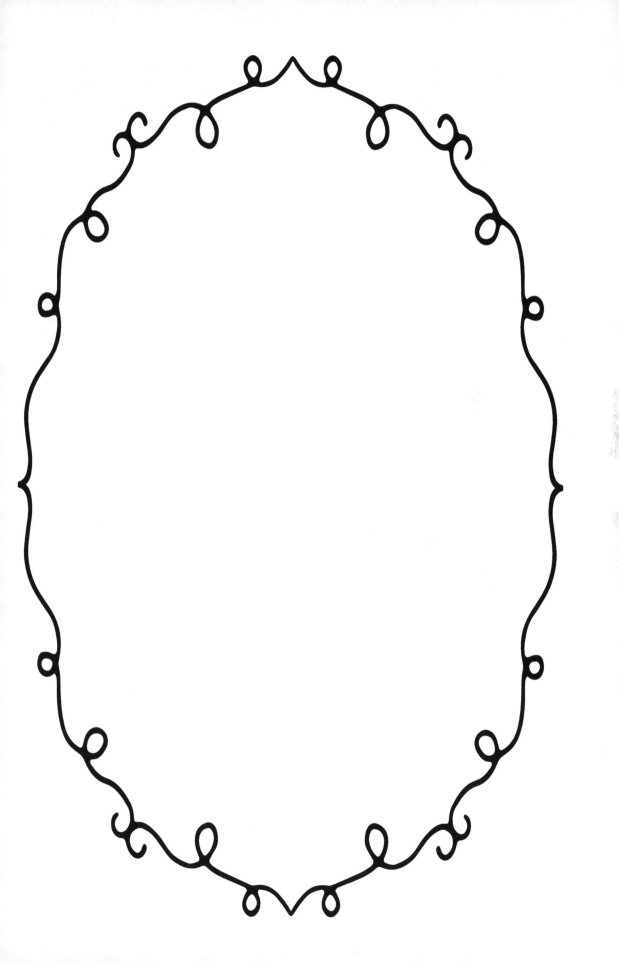

Today I am grateful for . . . .

_____
_____
_____
_____
_____
_____
_____
_____
_____
_____
_____
_____
_____
_____
_____

My favorite part of today was . . .

_____
_____
_____
_____
_____
_____
_____
_____
_____
_____

How are you Feeling?

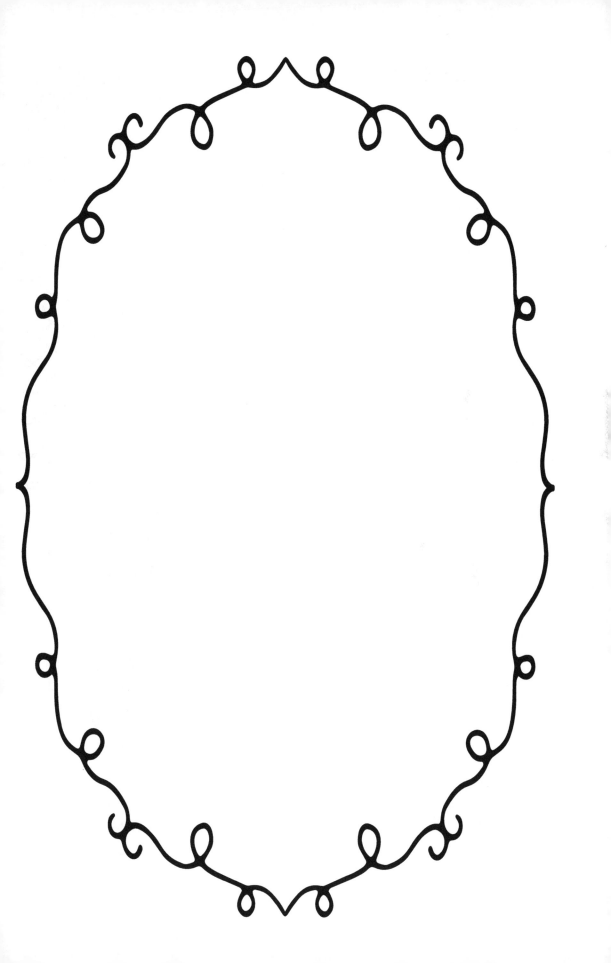

Today I am grateful for . . . .

My favorite part of today was . . .

How are you
Feeling?

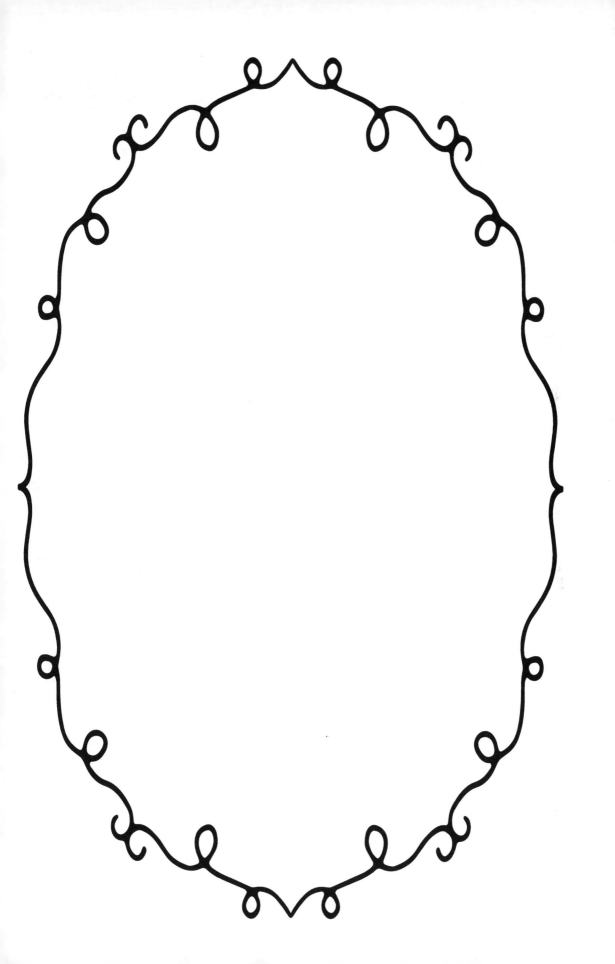

Today I am grateful for . . . .

My favorite part of today was . . .

How are you
Feeling?

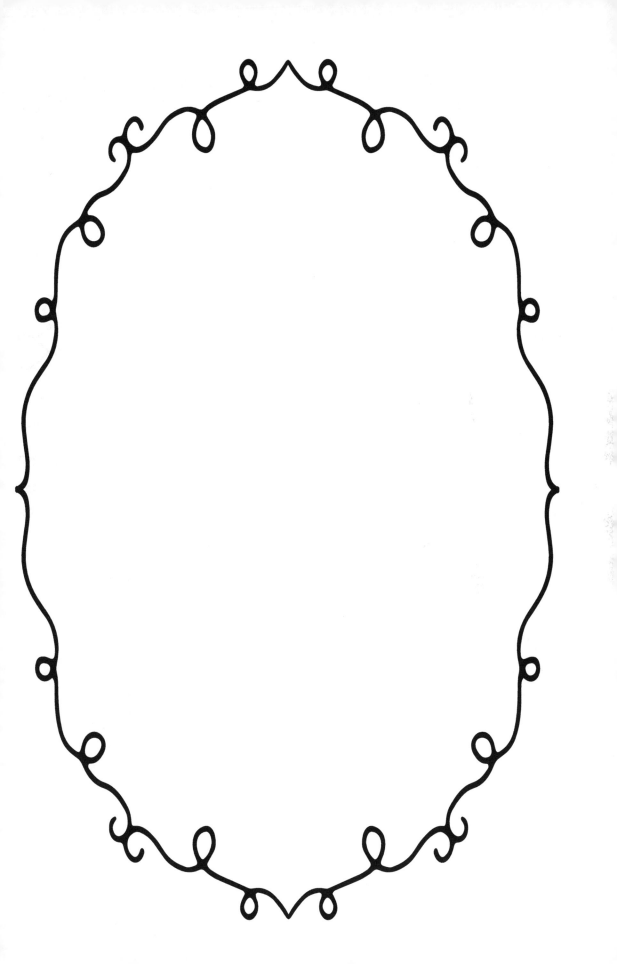

Today I am grateful for . . . .

_____
_____
_____
_____
_____
_____
_____
_____
_____
_____
_____
_____
_____
_____

My favorite part of today was . . .

_____
_____
_____
_____
_____
_____
_____
_____
_____
_____

How are you Feeling?

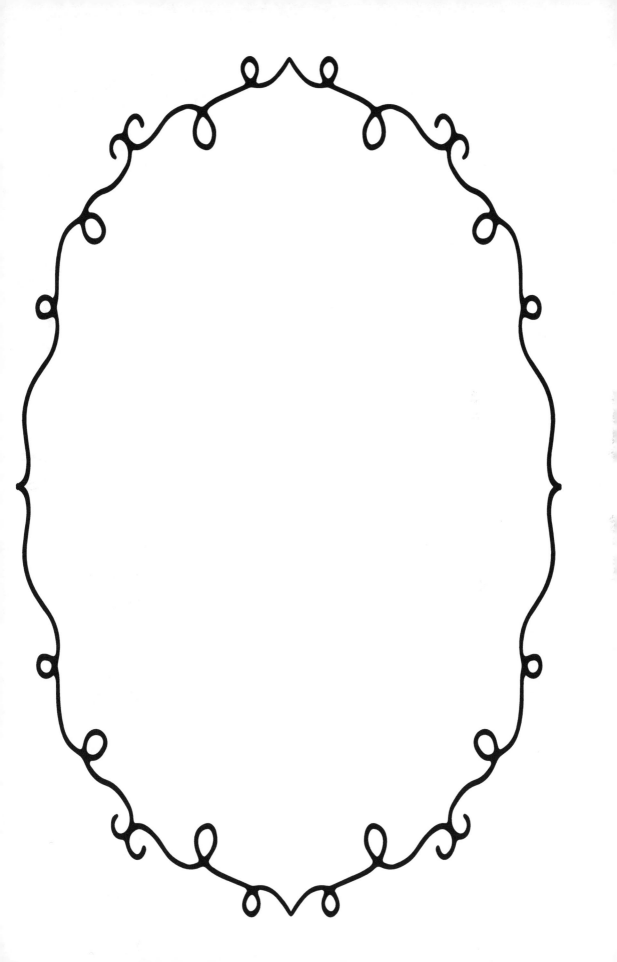

Today I am grateful for . . . .
_____
_____
_____
_____
_____
_____
_____
_____
_____
_____
_____
_____
_____
_____
_____

My favorite part of today was . . .
_____
_____
_____
_____
_____
_____
_____
_____
_____
_____
_____

How are you Feeling?

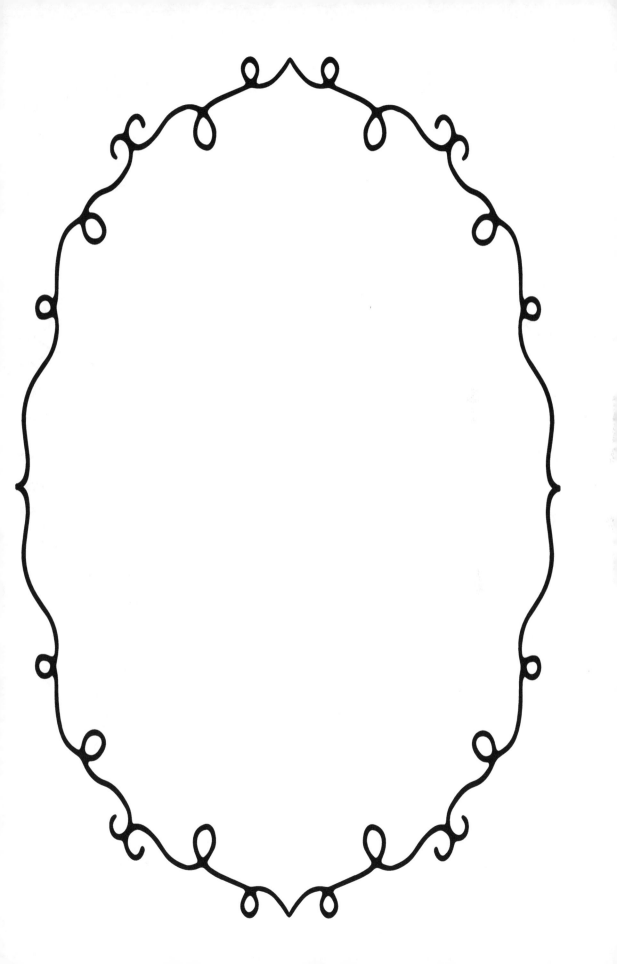

Today I am grateful for . . . .
_____
_____
_____
_____
_____
_____
_____
_____
_____
_____
_____
_____
_____
_____

My favorite part of today was . . .
_____
_____
_____
_____
_____
_____
_____
_____
_____
_____
_____

How are you
Feeling?

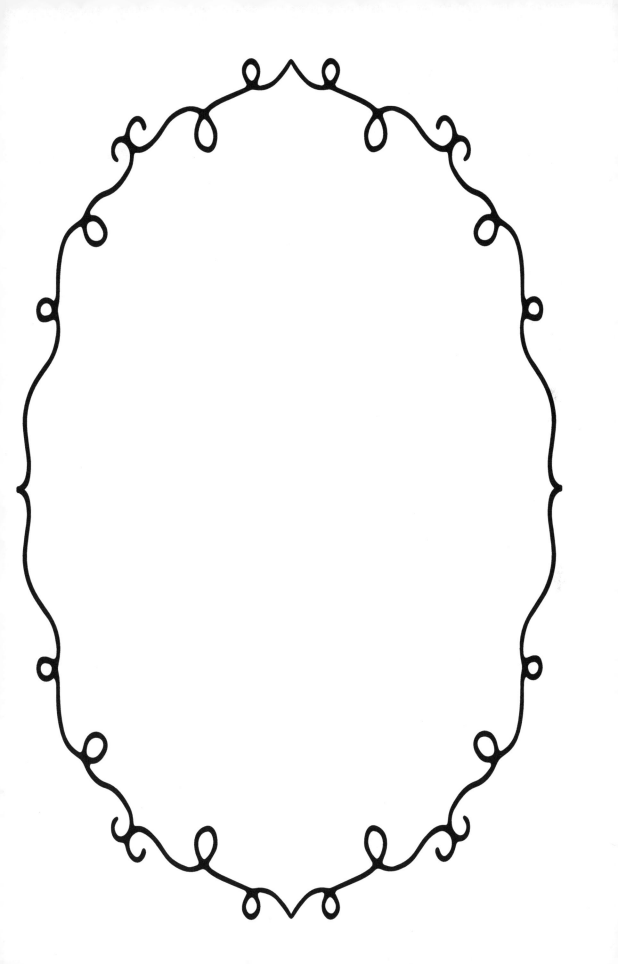

Today I am grateful for . . . .
_____
_____
_____
_____
_____
_____
_____
_____
_____
_____
_____
_____
_____
_____
_____
_____

My favorite part of today was . . .
_____
_____
_____
_____
_____
_____
_____
_____
_____
_____
_____

How are you
Feeling?

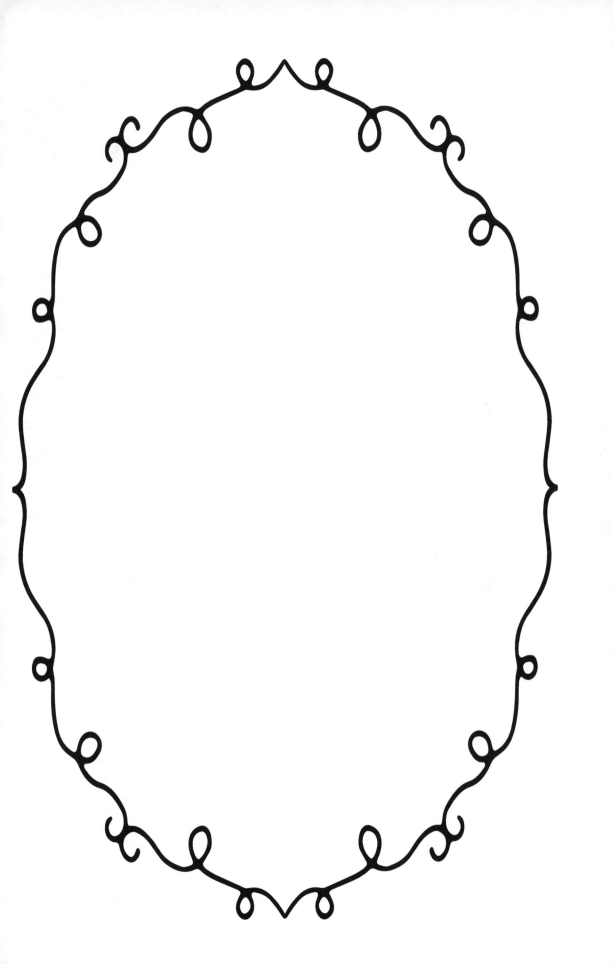

Today I am grateful for . . . .

My favorite part of today was . . .

How are you Feeling?

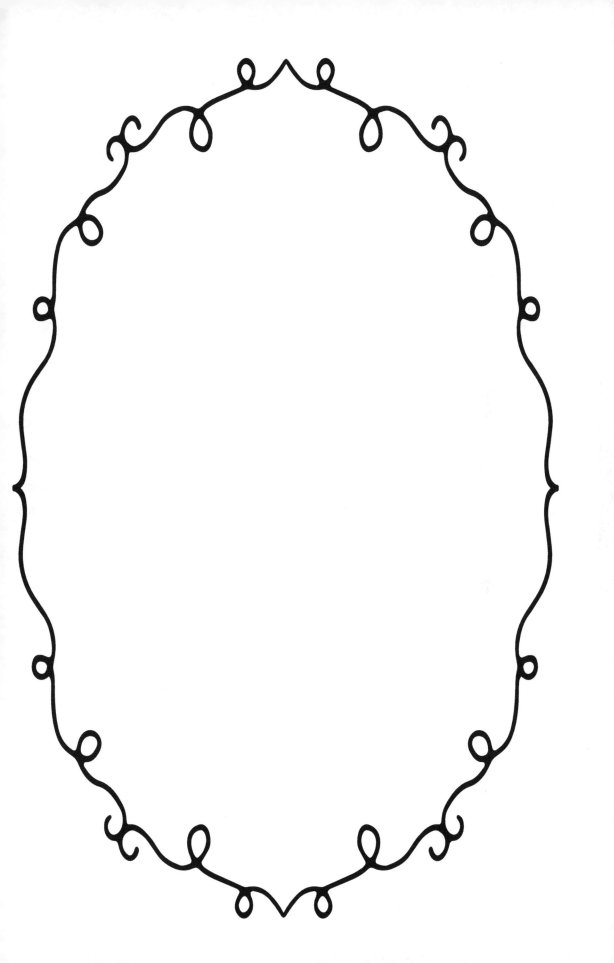

Today I am grateful for . . . .

_____
_____
_____
_____
_____
_____
_____
_____
_____
_____
_____
_____
_____

My favorite part of today was . . .

_____
_____
_____
_____
_____
_____
_____
_____
_____
_____
_____

How are you Feeling?

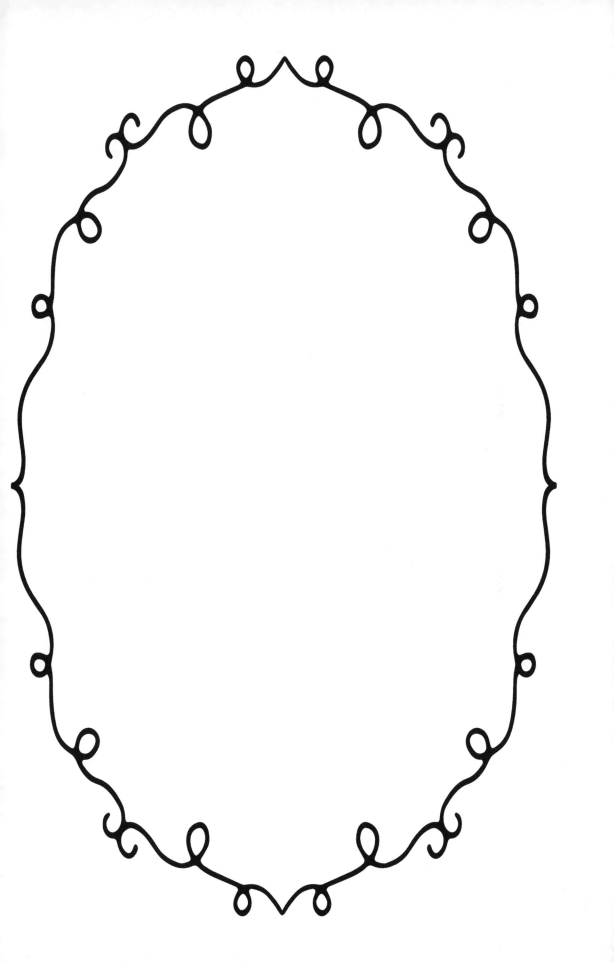

Today I am grateful for . . . .

My favorite part of today was . . .

How are you
Feeling?

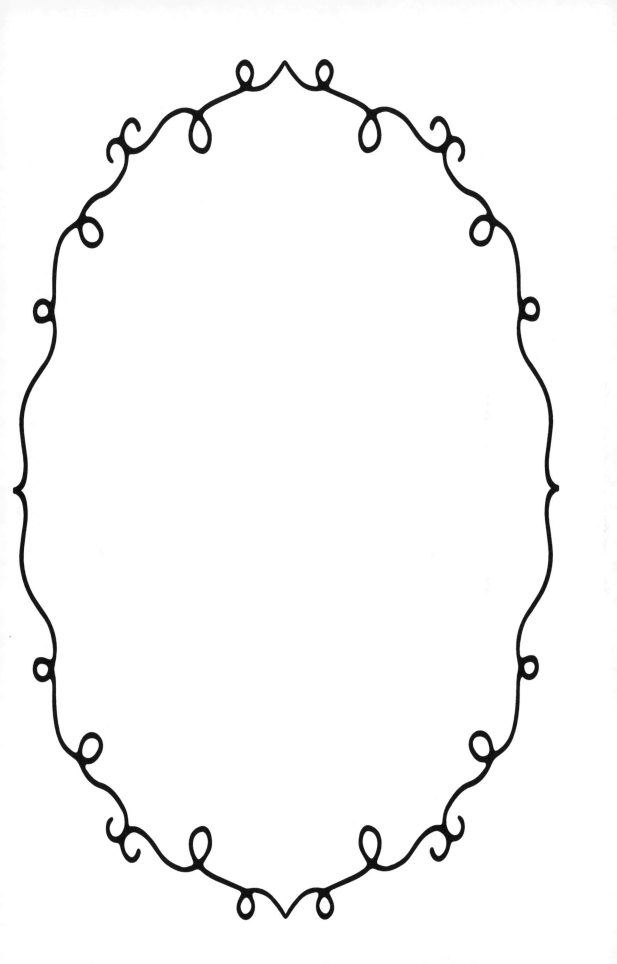

Today I am grateful for . . . .

My favorite part of today was . . .

How are you Feeling?

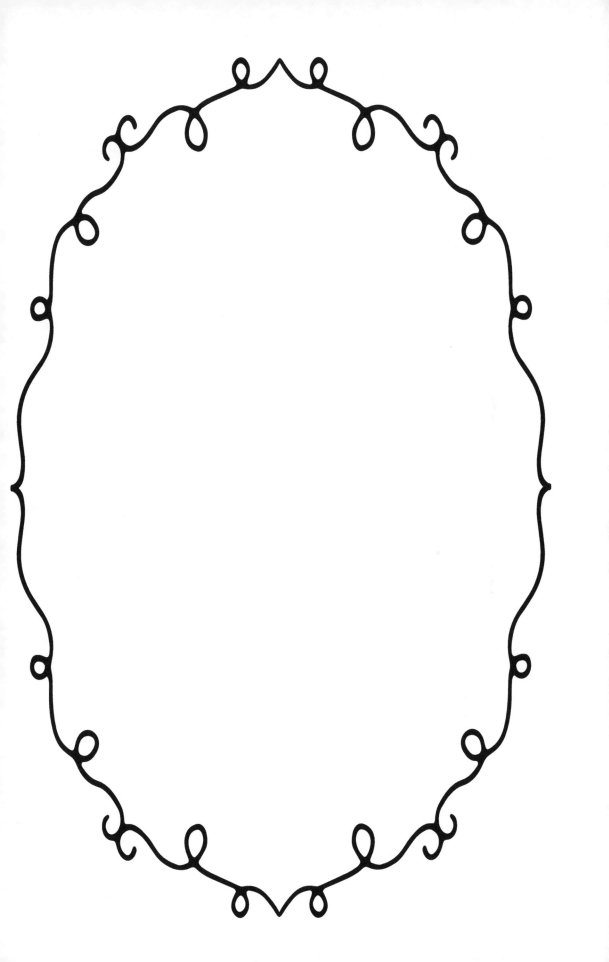

Today I am grateful for . . . .

My favorite part of today was . . .

How are you
Feeling?

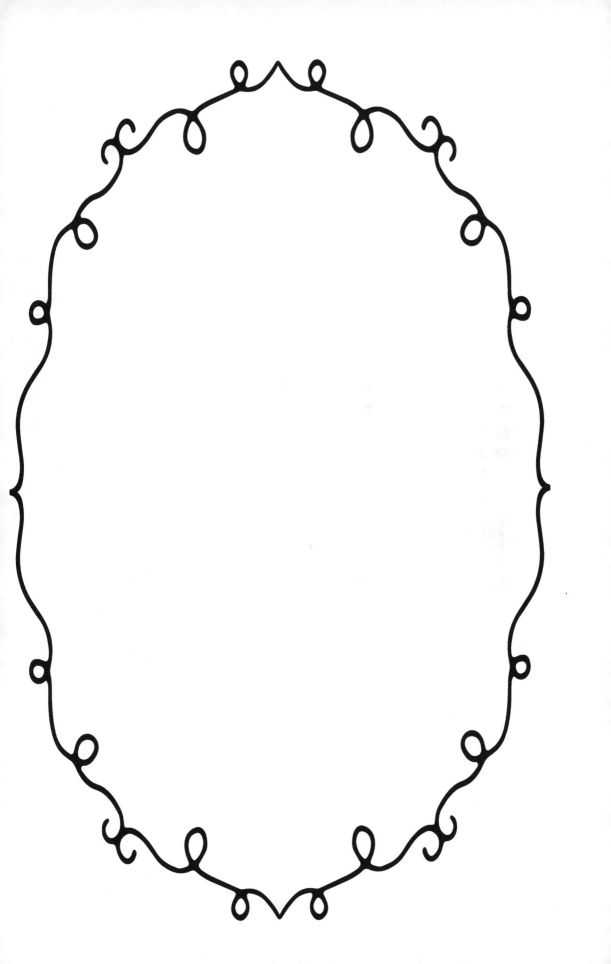

Today I am grateful for . . . .

My favorite part of today was . . .

How are you
Feeling?

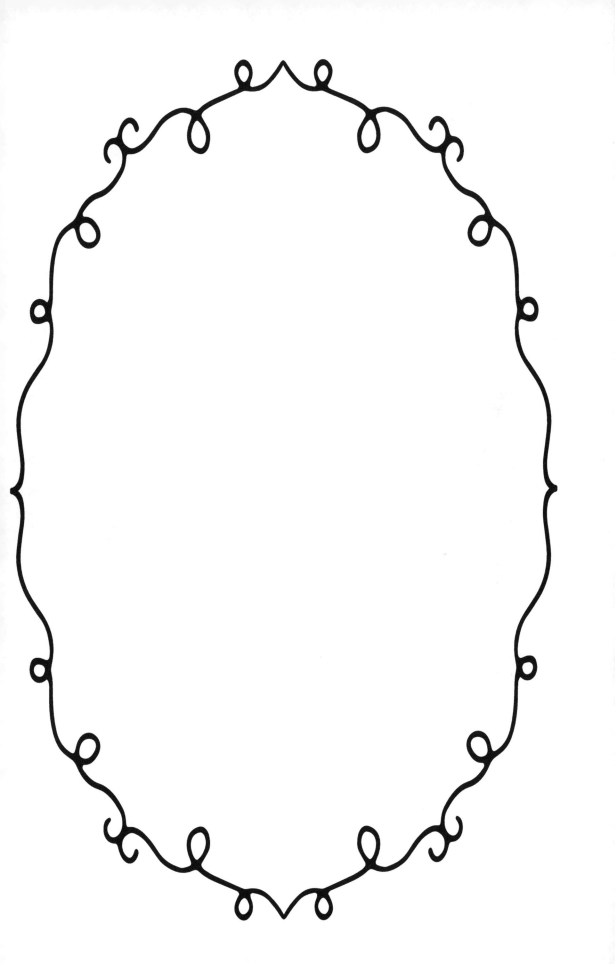

Today I am grateful for . . . .

My favorite part of today was . . .

How are you
Feeling?

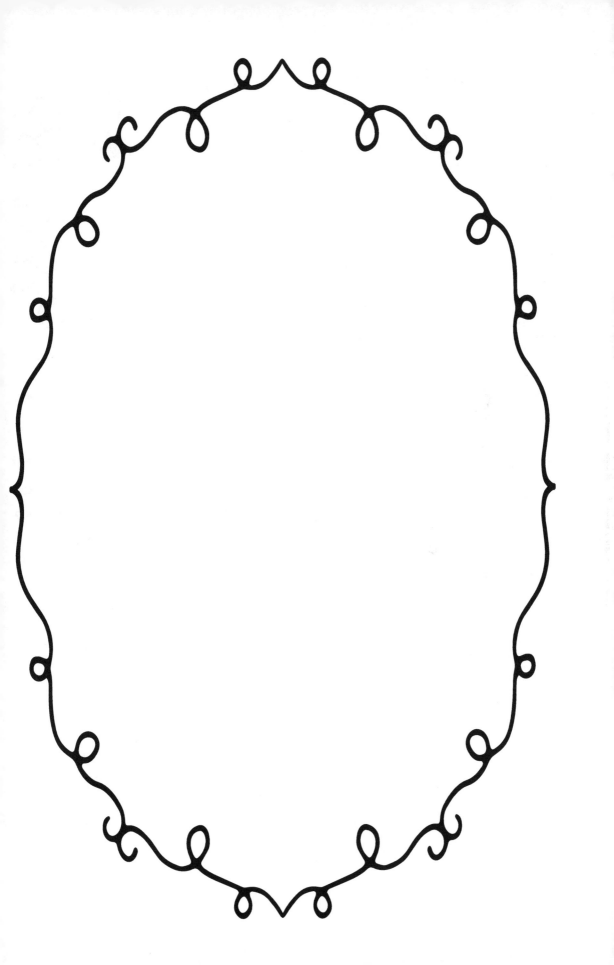

Today I am grateful for . . . .
_____
_____
_____
_____
_____
_____
_____
_____
_____
_____
_____
_____
_____

My favorite part of today was . . .
_____
_____
_____
_____
_____
_____
_____
_____
_____
_____

How are you
Feeling?

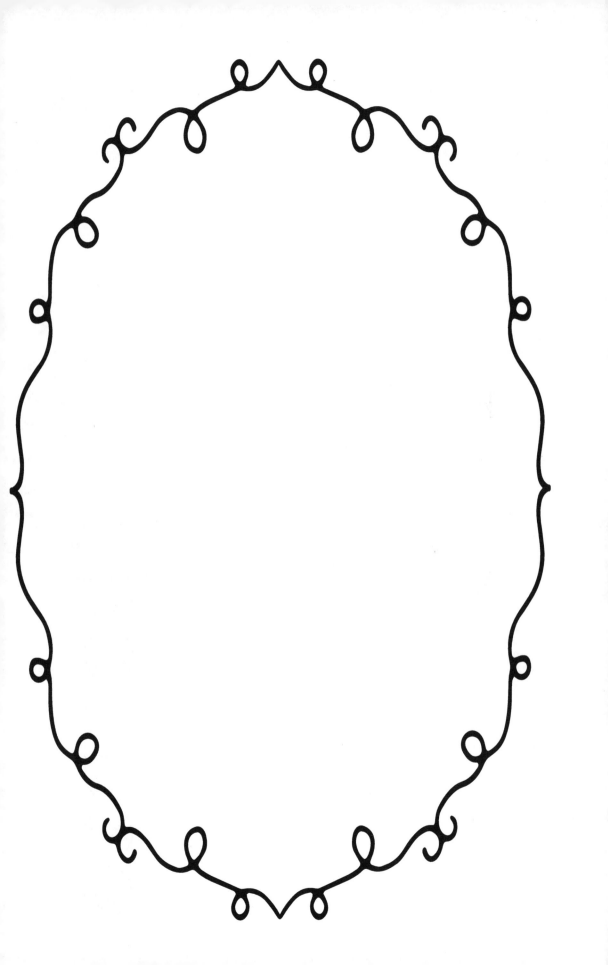

Today I am grateful for . . . .

_____
_____
_____
_____
_____
_____
_____
_____
_____
_____
_____
_____
_____
_____

My favorite part of today was . . .

_____
_____
_____
_____
_____
_____
_____
_____
_____
_____
_____
_____

How are you Feeling?

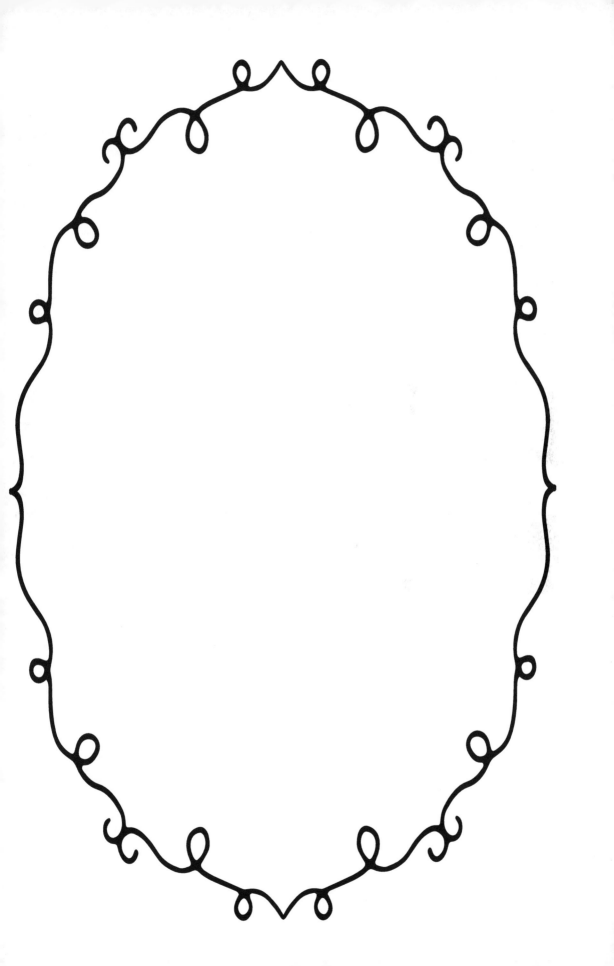

Today I am grateful for . . . .

My favorite part of today was . . .

How are you Feeling?

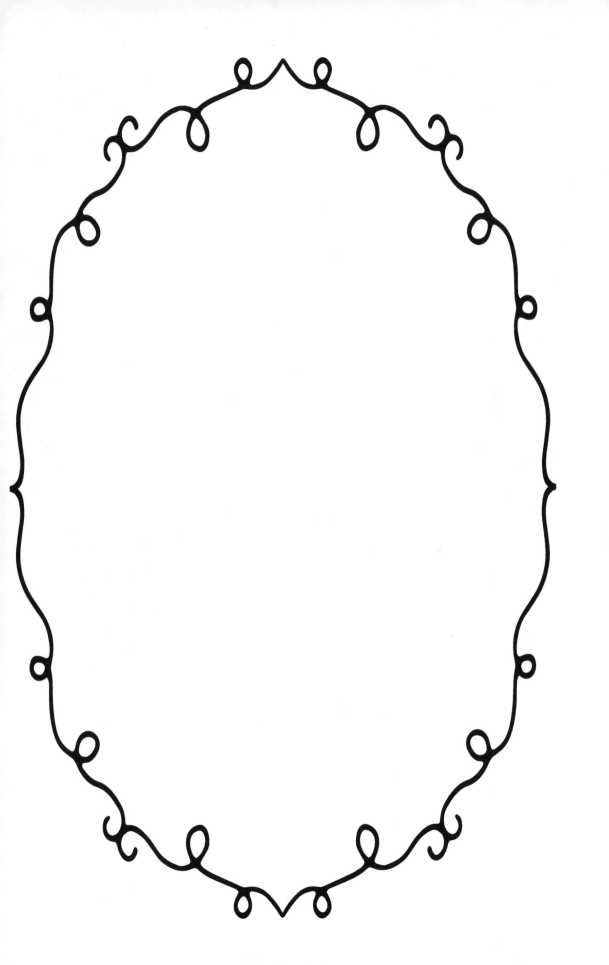

Today I am grateful for . . . .

_____

_____

_____

_____

_____

_____

_____

_____

_____

_____

_____

_____

_____

My favorite part of today was . . .

_____

_____

_____

_____

_____

_____

_____

_____

_____

_____

How are you Feeling?

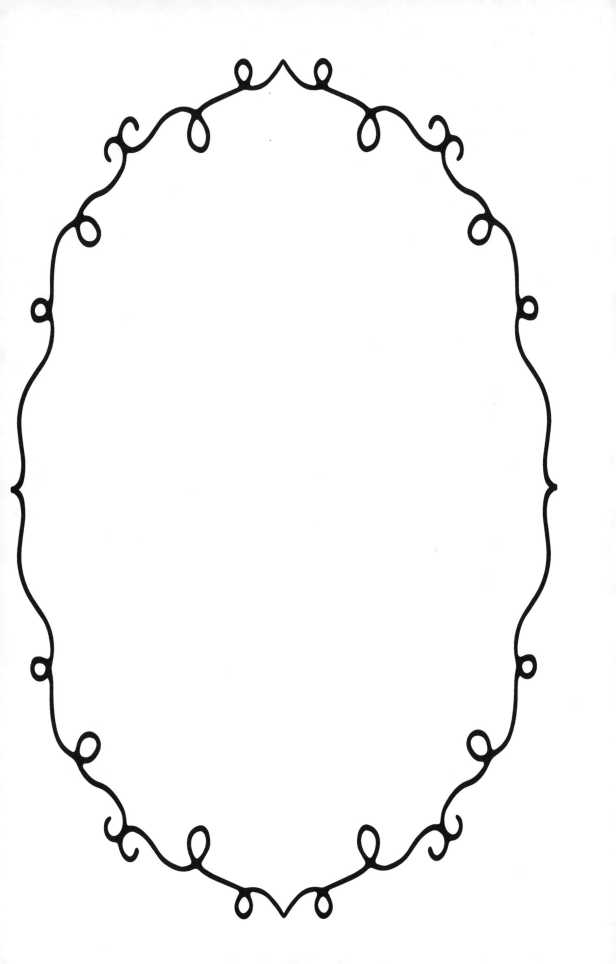

Today I am grateful for . . . .

My favorite part of today was . . .

How are you Feeling?

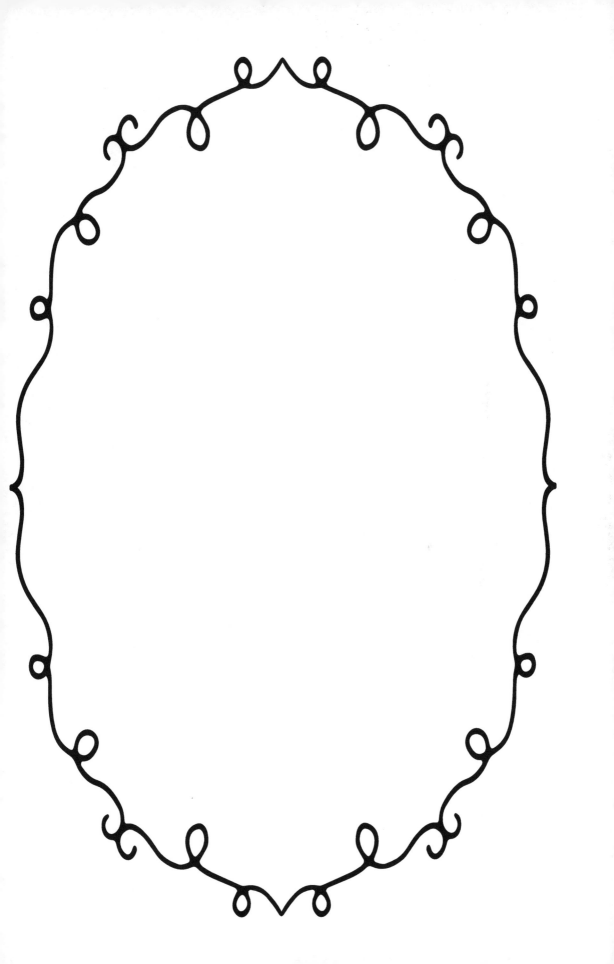

Today I am grateful for . . . .

_____
_____
_____
_____
_____
_____
_____
_____
_____
_____
_____
_____
_____
_____

My favorite part of today was . . .

_____
_____
_____
_____
_____
_____
_____
_____
_____
_____
_____
_____

How are you Feeling?

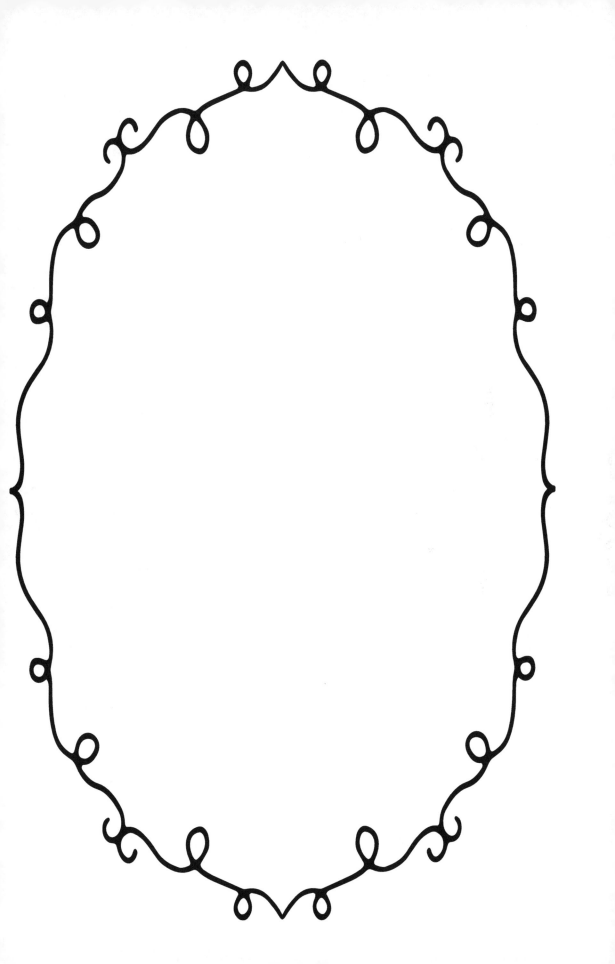

Today I am grateful for . . . .

My favorite part of today was . . .

How are you
Feeling?

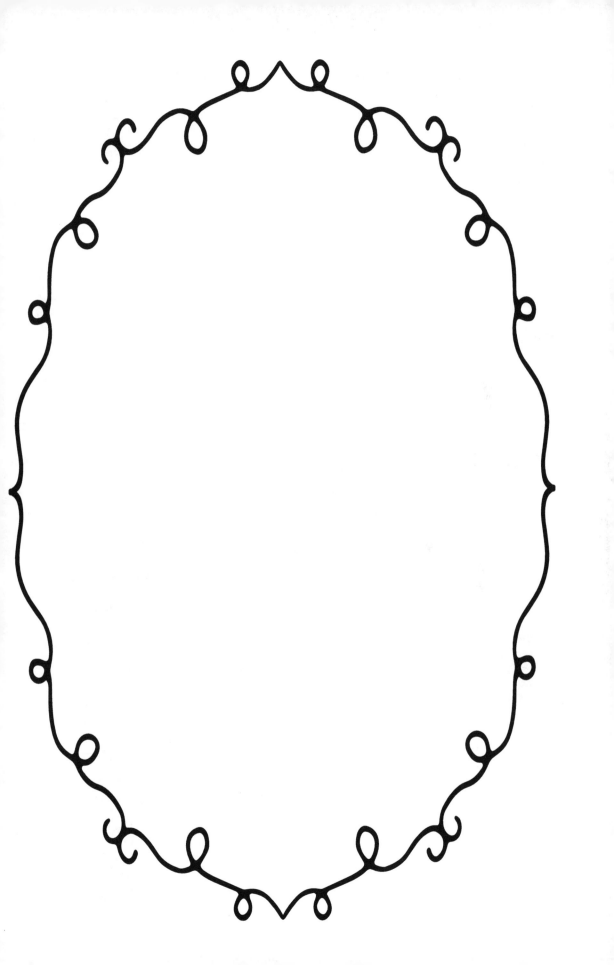

Today I am grateful for . . . .

My favorite part of today was . . .

How are you Feeling?

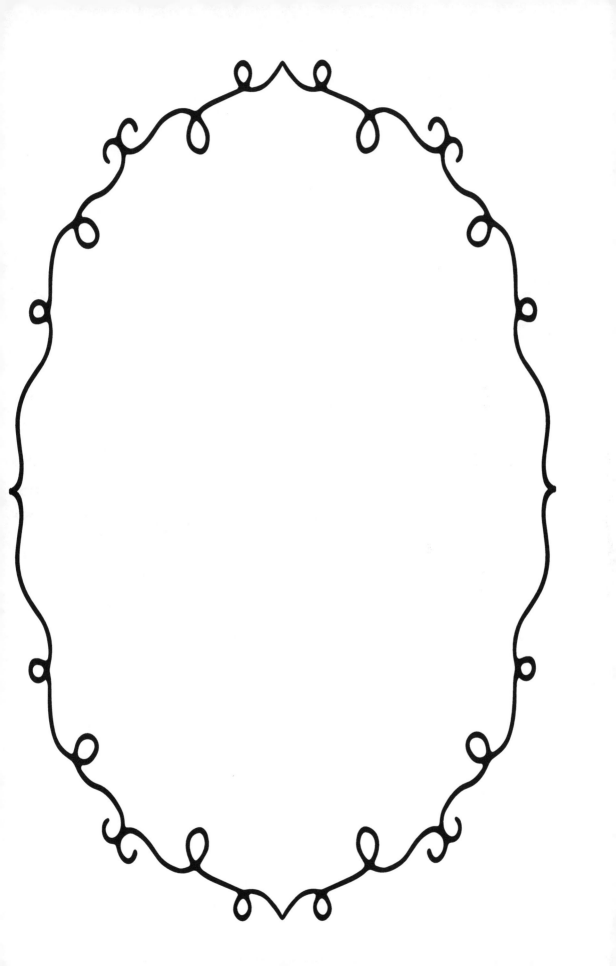

Today I am grateful for . . . .

_____
_____
_____
_____
_____
_____
_____
_____
_____
_____
_____
_____
_____

My favorite part of today was . . .

_____
_____
_____
_____
_____
_____
_____
_____
_____
_____
_____

How are you Feeling?

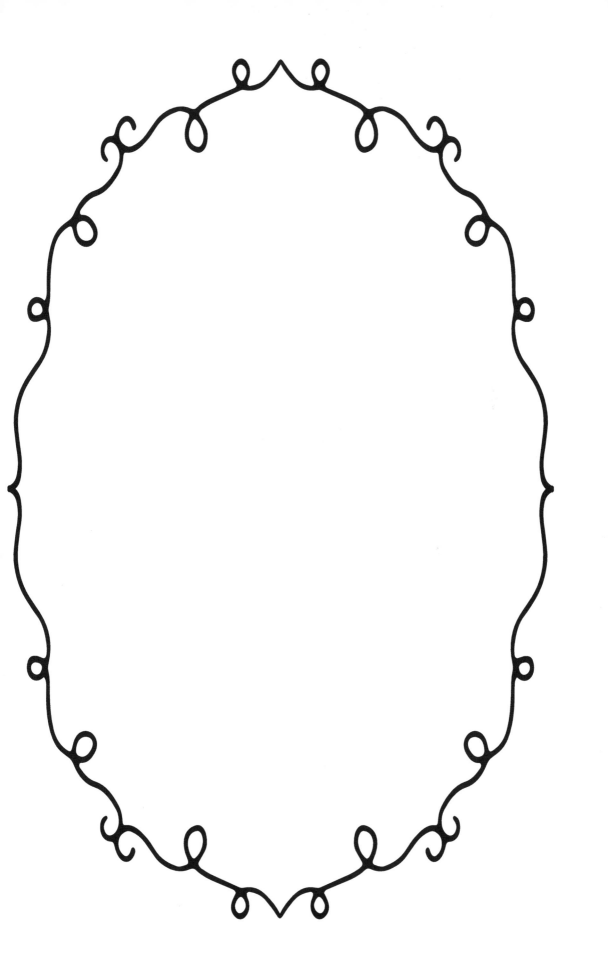

Today I am grateful for . . . .

My favorite part of today was . . .

How are you
Feeling?

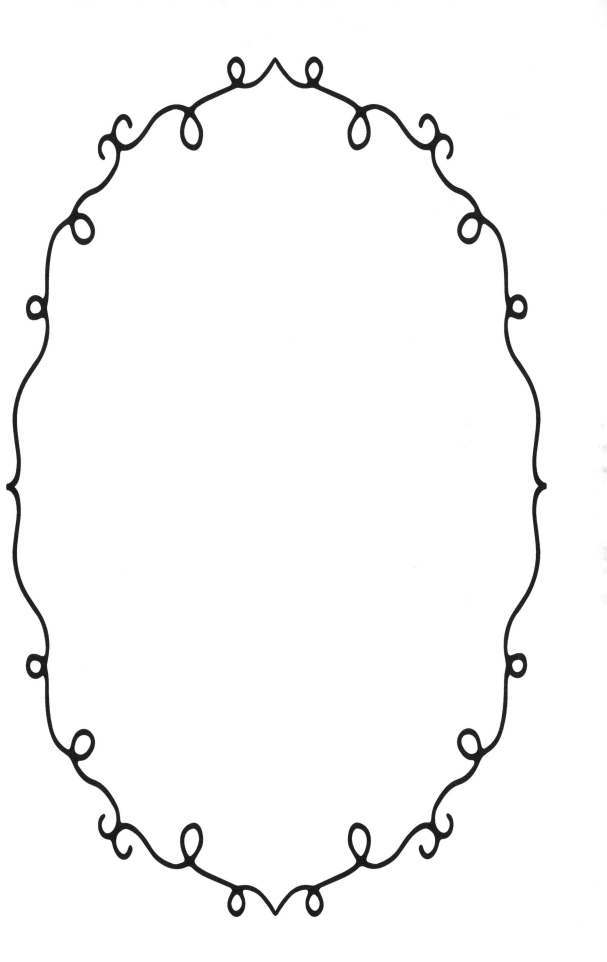

Today I am grateful for . . . .

My favorite part of today was . . .

How are you
Feeling?

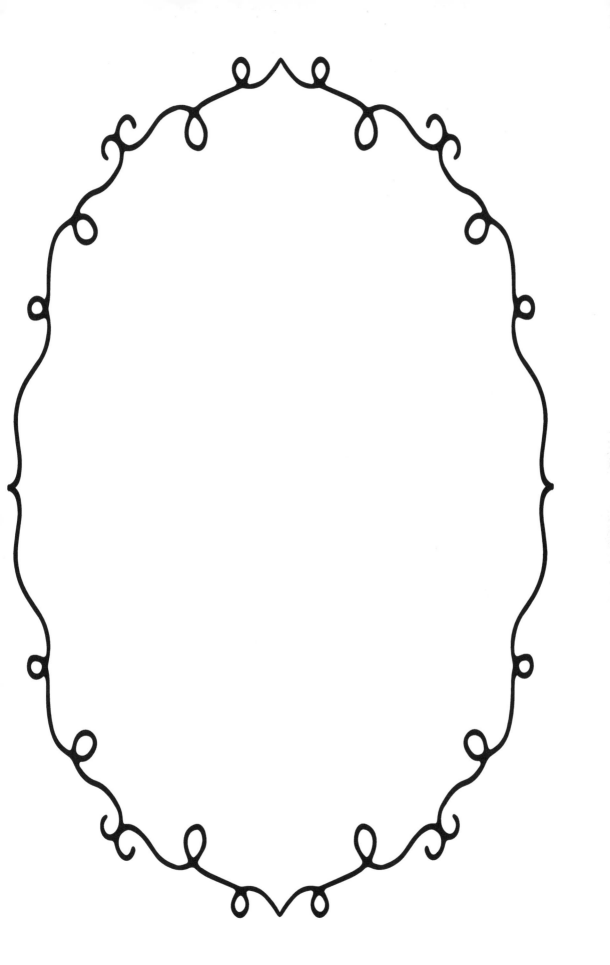

Today I am grateful for . . . .

My favorite part of today was . . .

How are you
Feeling?

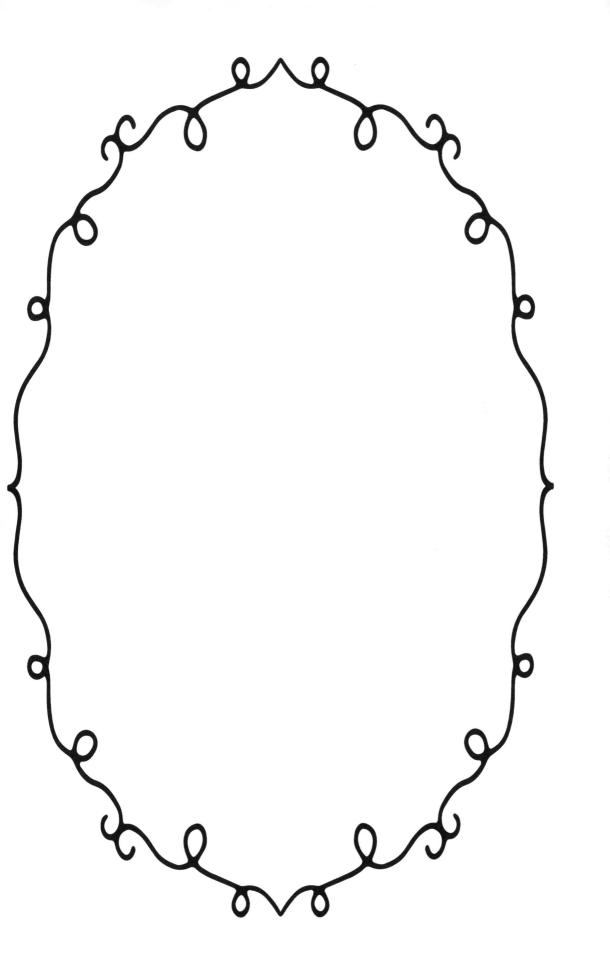

Today I am grateful for . . . .

_____
_____
_____
_____
_____
_____
_____
_____
_____
_____
_____
_____
_____
_____
_____
_____

My favorite part of today was . . .

_____
_____
_____
_____
_____
_____
_____
_____
_____
_____
_____
_____

How are you Feeling?

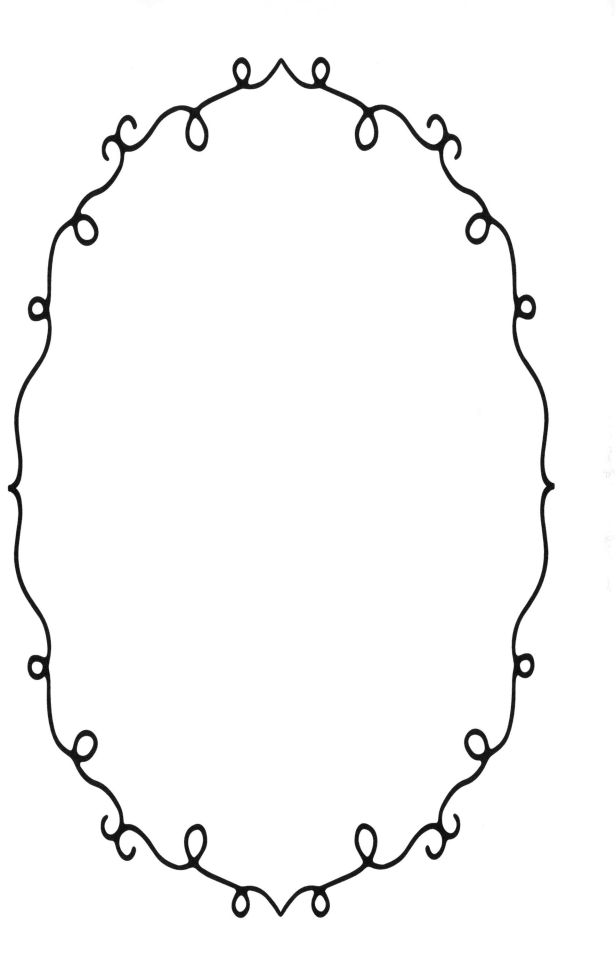

Today I am grateful for . . . .

My favorite part of today was . . .

How are you Feeling?

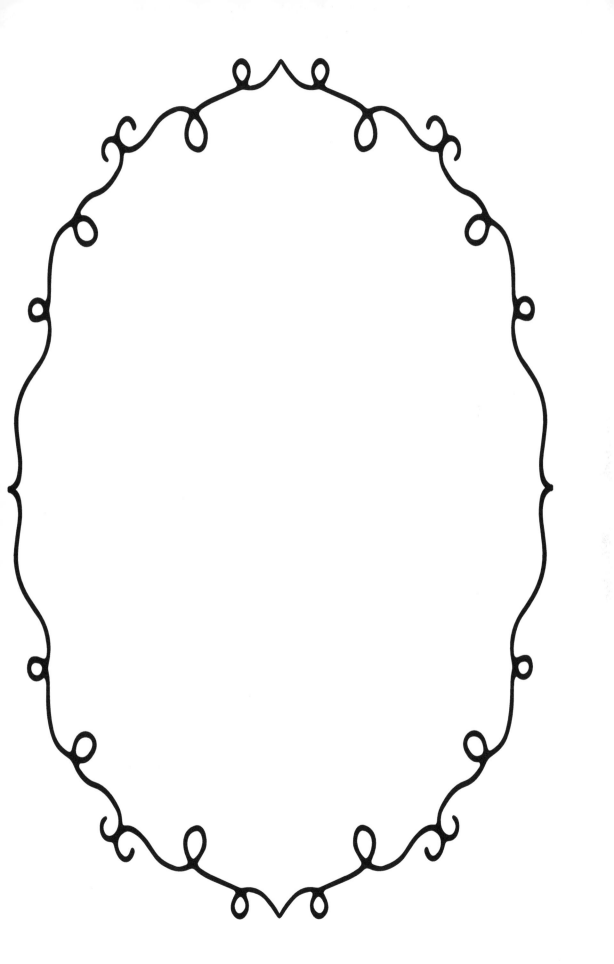

Today I am grateful for . . . .

My favorite part of today was . . .

How are you
Feeling?

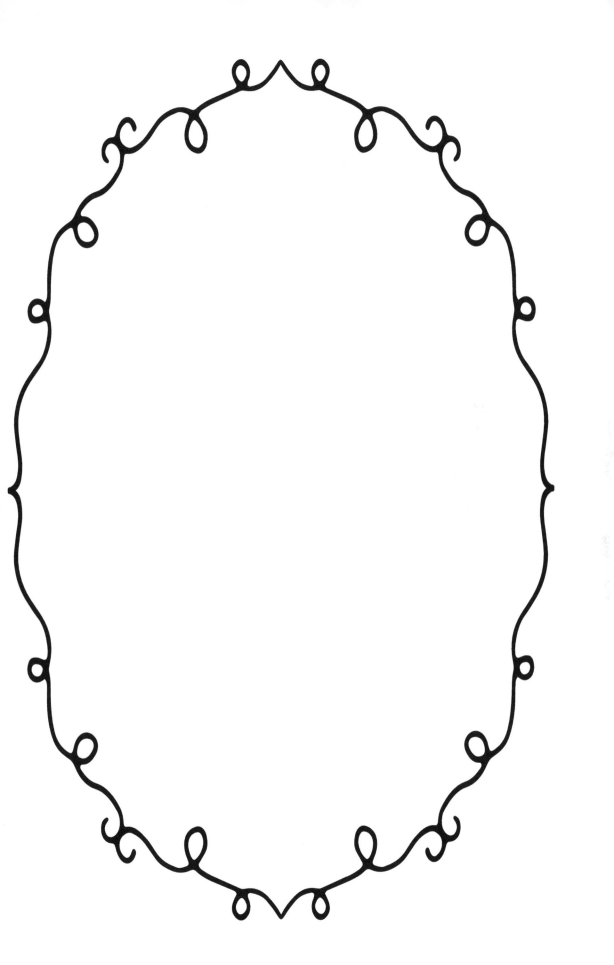

Today I am grateful for . . . .

My favorite part of today was . . .

How are you
Feeling?

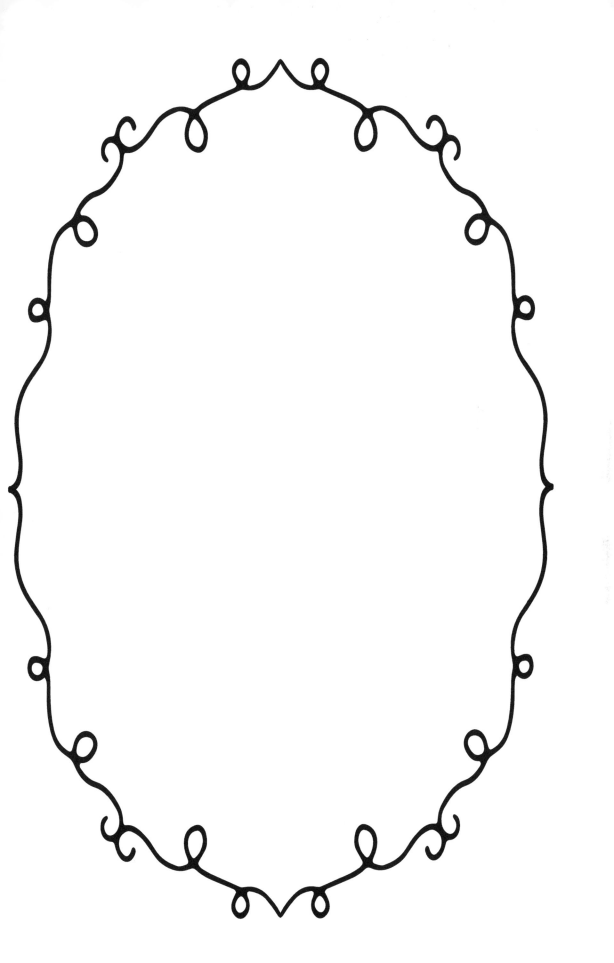

Today I am grateful for . . . .

My favorite part of today was . . .

How are you
Feeling?

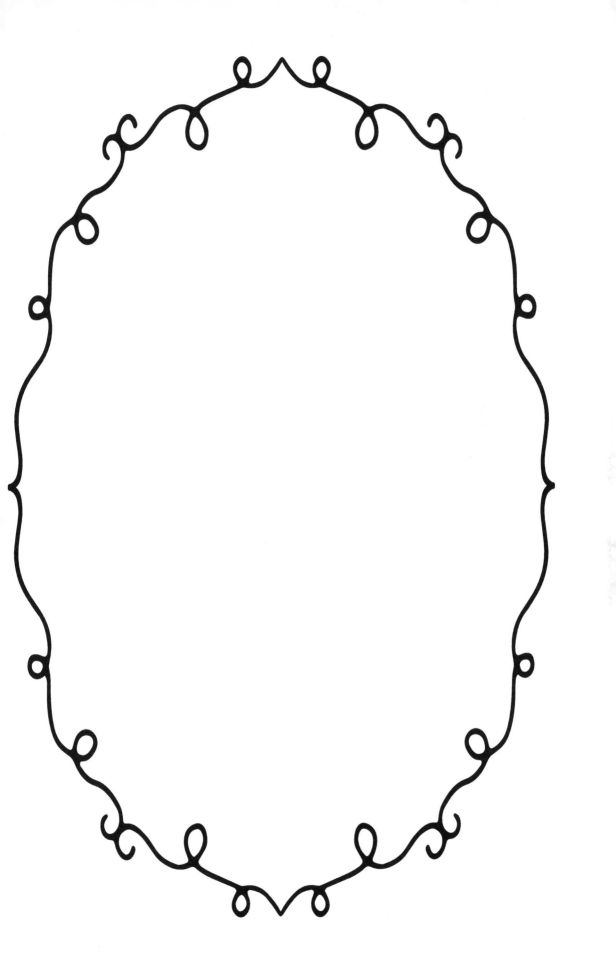

Today I am grateful for . . . .

_____
_____
_____
_____
_____
_____
_____
_____
_____
_____
_____
_____
_____
_____
_____

My favorite part of today was . . .

_____
_____
_____
_____
_____
_____
_____
_____
_____
_____
_____
_____

How are you Feeling?

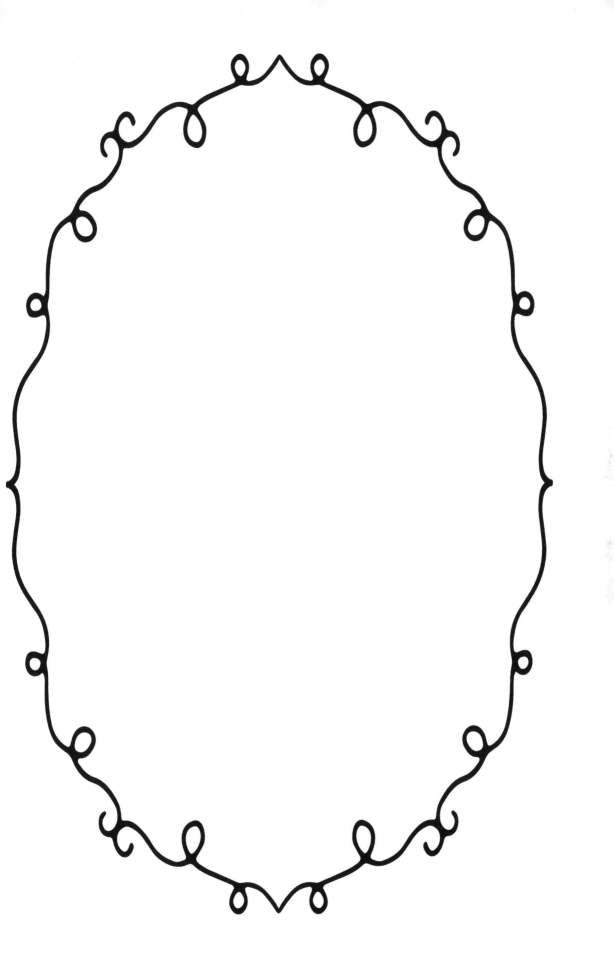

Today I am grateful for . . . .

My favorite part of today was . . .

How are you
Feeling?

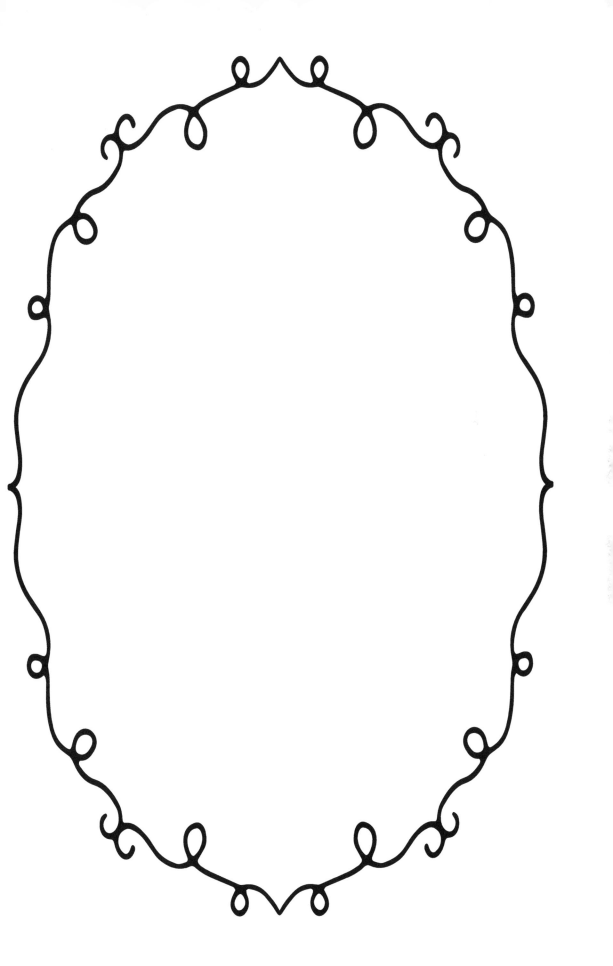

Today I am grateful for . . . .

_____
_____
_____
_____
_____
_____
_____
_____
_____
_____
_____
_____
_____
_____

My favorite part of today was . . .

_____
_____
_____
_____
_____
_____
_____
_____
_____
_____
_____
_____

How are you Feeling?

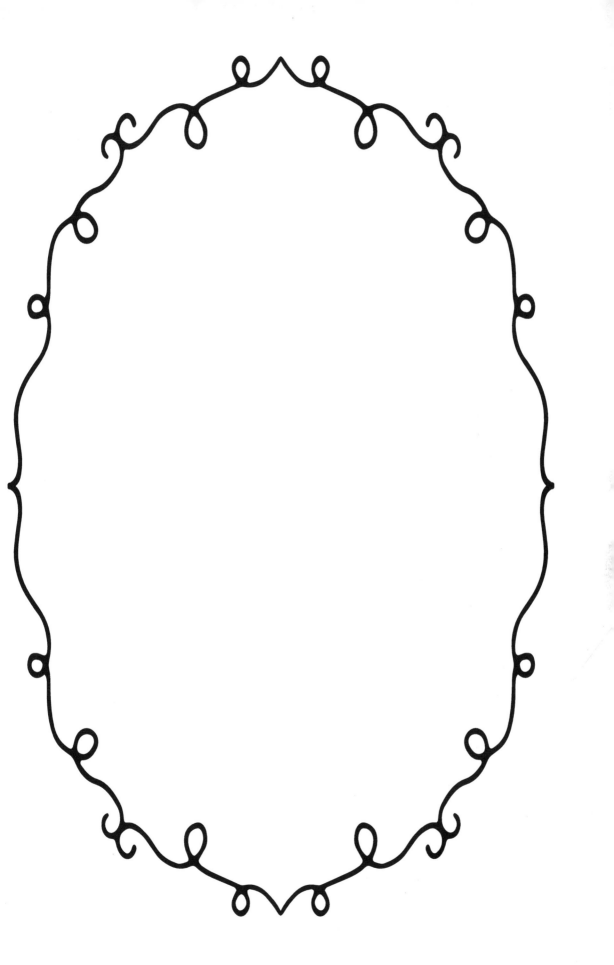

Made in the USA
Columbia, SC
08 December 2017